They Made All the Difference

They Made All the Difference

Life-Changing Stories from Jesuit High Schools

EILEEN WIRTH, PhD

LOYOLAPRESS.
CHICAGO

LOYOLAPRESS.

3441 N. ASHLAND AVENUE
CHICAGO, ILLINOIS 60657
(800) 621-1008
WWW.LOYOLABOOKS.ORG

Cover design by Adam Moroschan
Interior design by Mia Basile

Library of Congress Cataloging-in-Publication Data
Wirth, Eileen.
    They made all the difference : life-changing stories from Jesuit high schools / Eileen Wirth.
        p. cm.
    Includes bibliographical references.
    ISBN-13: 978-0-8294-2168-2
    ISBN-10: 0-8294-2168-8
    1. Catholic high schools—United States. 2. Catholic Church—Education—United States. I. Title.
    LC501.W6 2007
    371.071'2--dc22
                                        2007012311

Printed in the United States of America
07 08 09 10 11 12 M-V 10 9 8 7 6 5 4 3 2 1

To my mother, Kathleen McGowen Wirth, for opening the world far beyond our farm through books, books, and more books; for refusing to raise her daughters according to conventional 1950s limits; and for modeling volunteerism, especially in our schools, without which I would never have gotten involved at Creighton Prep or come to write this book.

Mother exemplifies the Ignatian ideal: she's lived as a woman for others and made this world a better place. She is my hero.

Contents

Jesuit education is the finest education you can get in the world. The religious part of a Jesuit education is based on our common faith and the Spiritual Exercises. If you say "Spiritual Exercises" or "prayer of generosity" to any student at any Jesuit school, they'll know what that is. A year and a half ago, I was wearing a Jesuit sweatshirt with AMDG in an elevator. A man saw my sweatshirt and said, "I went to a Jesuit high school. I went to Tampa Jesuit." Another time I was having a conversation at a camp at Stanford with a kid in my dorm hall. The kid was going to Boston College High School. The same thing happened. We shared our stories. We all have these common stories. We can tell them to complete strangers and we know they will understand, because they are our families.

Ian Gunn, class of '07,
Jesuit High School, New Orleans

Introduction: Ignatian Journeys

The Jesuits were the keepers of a flame too long kept in a black cloak. The flame caught on fire with people wearing other-colored clothing. Now they are on fire. Ignatian spirituality works for lay folk. Ignatius was a layman when he developed the Spiritual Exercises. This is a great thing.

> Fr. Walter Deye, SJ, president,
> St. Xavier High School

Thirty-five years ago, the nation's Jesuit high schools were reeling from an identity crisis. Jesuits were leaving both the schools and the Society; social action ministries seemed more relevant than teaching high school. Should the Jesuits continue to run high schools for upper- and middle-class students or focus on serving the poor?

Simultaneously, urban riots slashed enrollments at some inner-city Jesuit schools, and single-sex education seemed to some to be a chauvinistic anachronism. Replacing Jesuits with lay faculty raised tuition. Some of the nation's best Catholic high schools were in danger.

Fast-forward to 2006. The "long black line" of Jesuits is gone, with just a handful of priests and brothers remaining in most of the forty-nine American Jesuit high schools. However, the Society of Jesus is committed to its high schools, because Jesuits now realize that they provide outstanding opportunities for the spiritual formation of young people, says Fr. Ralph Metts, SJ, president of the Jesuit Secondary Education Association (JSEA). AMDG still rules at today's thriving schools. Consider these developments:

- Inner-city Jesuit Cristo Rey high schools, where low-income students work for their tuition, are opening rapidly. Two were added to the network in 2006, with more planned.
- Most of the traditional Jesuit high schools are at capacity, with competitive enrollments. This includes inner-city schools once threatened with closing.
- The schools are raising at least four hundred million dollars in capital campaigns alone to upgrade campuses and enhance endowments/financial aid.
- Jesuit schools all over the country are still academically and athletically elite.

What lies behind this turnaround?

That's what I sought to discover in writing this book. After teaching at Creighton University, in Omaha, for fifteen years and writing about Catholic high schools, I also wanted to better understand *why* so many Jesuit high school alums say these years were definitive. That's not what most people say about their high school experience. Finally, I assumed I would find great stories like those Tim Russert tells in his book *Big Russ & Me*—stories that resonate with anyone who loves Jesuit education, as I do.

This book takes you behind the scenes at today's Jesuit high schools. If you ever wondered how your old disciplinarian knew when you were up to something, you'll find out here. If you're curious about how the schools raise so much money, a development director explains it. If you want to be inspired by teachers who give their lives to change young lives, this book will do that. You'll also meet alums serving others in all sorts of interesting ways because of the impact of their high schools.

To research this book, I visited Jesuit high schools in New York City; Washington, DC; Houston (when students and staff from New

Orleans were there); Chicago; Indianapolis; San Francisco; Kansas City; the Pine Ridge Reservation; and, of course, Omaha. I also did phone interviews with officials of the Jesuit Secondary Education Association (JSEA), provincial assistants for secondary education, and personnel and alumni from numerous other schools. I read everything I could get my hands on, including the Web sites of all the Jesuit high schools. Countless people shared their stories with me.

They were all the same story, really. Everyone connected with Jesuit high schools seems caught up in the demanding but loving educational vision of St. Ignatius—a genius if ever there was one. The schools base everything they do on Ignatian spirituality. It is the key to their success, and it is now embraced by lay faculty as fervently as it is by the remaining Jesuits. This book shows how Ignatian spirituality guides Jesuit high schools to succeed in everything from football to freshman retreats.

Jesuit High Schools: Not for the Faint of Heart

Jesuit high schools enforce standards and rules. They don't pander to students, no matter how high the tuition. They'll survive if you leave, thank you. Although a third are coed, they exude a masculinity that is traceable to St. Ignatius. *Cura personalis*, or "care for the person," means caring with a purpose—knowing students so well that they can be sent on missions to serve others. It's a challenging and demanding form of love.

While most Jesuit high school alums seem to be passionately proud of their alma maters, some have bitter memories. They experienced discipline that went too far, they hated conforming to the rules, or they felt like nonentities because they didn't play sports. Some schools expelled students because they wouldn't conform to the rules, and those students went on to notable careers.

Some people are turned off by the wealth and elitism of many of the schools, or they are jealous of their success and, yes, arrogance. Some parents question if the financial sacrifice is worth it. Internal critics say that Jesuit high schools do a good job of stressing service but don't do nearly enough to get students to connect feeding the homeless at a shelter with working for social change. They want the schools to take that next step toward the vision of former superior general Pedro Arrupe, SJ, of solidarity for and with the poor.

I can sympathize with the critics and the doubters. I sent my son to Creighton Prep because our parish high school closed suddenly when he was an eighth grader. I imposed Prep on him during this crisis, although later he was grateful. At first, Prep seemed formidable rather than hospitable to newcomers trying to crack its code. However, during my son's sophomore year, two incidents showed me its heart.

In the first, the disciplinarian punished my son for violating a significant rule. By handling the incident with firmness, wisdom, and compassion, David Laughlin, now president of St. Louis University High School, taught my son more about accountability in one day than he could have learned in a year of lectures. My son, now an air force sergeant, grew up a year in one month. You'll meet Laughlin in the chapter on discipline.

A few months later, Jesse Mans, our neighbor and a Prep sophomore, was diagnosed with cancer and died soon after. A counselor from Prep called students to find out which boys who had attended St. Cecilia's Grade School with him would need extra care. Prep honored Jesse at his class's baccalaureate Mass and included his name (with a cross next to it) on the graduation list. I have never forgotten this sensitivity.

At the same baccalaureate Mass, history teacher and coach Greg Glenn, whom the class had elected as speaker, celebrated the essence of Prep and all Jesuit high schools when he said that the boys had come together as strangers but were leaving as valued members of a community. Whether they were athletes or in Academic Decathlon, band members or environmental activists, someone had nurtured them. Someone would miss them next year. But now it was time to go forth as men for others to serve the world.

The Jesuit High School World

Jesuit schools enroll about forty thousand students nationwide and have about four hundred thousand alums. They "share a worldview, a spirituality, and a particular way of doing education," says Fr. Thomas Merkel, SJ, president of Creighton Prep and a former JSEA board chair. They believe they are doing critically important work in motivating bright young people to serve God and the world, especially the poor.

Formerly, Jesuit and lay faculty lived in "different worlds" and played different roles in the schools, but JSEA helped break down these barriers through Ignatian leadership training programs. Now all faculty are expected to promote Ignatian mission and identity, and most do. At every school I visited, Jesuits joked that some of their lay colleagues are "more Jesuit than the Jesuits."

According to Merkel, the Jesuit schools' linkage through the Society of Jesus and JSEA has had an impact on the following areas:

- **Spirituality, Vision, and Mission.** In the process of teaching students, Jesuit high schools are preparing each student to carry out a mission to change the world for the good. This leads schools to demand extraordinary commitment from their teachers and their students and creates a sense of national and even international community.

- **Vocabulary.** Jesuit high schools use a common vocabulary to explain who they are, what they do, and what makes them distinctive. They use the same key phrases in the same way all over the country. People joke, "Do you speak Ignatian?"
- **Goals/Expectations.** American Jesuit high schools have agreed on common goals for their graduates—open to growth, intellectually competent, religious, loving, and committed to doing justice—and follow common operating guidelines developed through JSEA.
- **Identity.** The common spirituality and goals give Jesuit high schools a shared identity. They operate like branches or franchises of a national brand, a tremendous asset in a mobile society.
- **Credibility.** Jesuit schools have a common 450-year-old track record of educational and spiritual success that benefits every local affiliate.
- **Pedagogy.** The early European Jesuits developed the *Ratio Studiorum*, the world's first educational master plan, by sharing insights on best practices. Today's schools also share good ideas and develop common practices, strengthening their common identity.
- **Networking/Problem Solving.** JSEA workshops and retreats introduce administrators and faculty members to their peers at other schools so they can help one another develop nationally consistent approaches to teaching, discipline, and problem solving.
- **Hiring.** Jesuit high schools hire teachers based on similar spiritual and educational criteria: teachers who are experts in their fields, passionate about teaching, willing to devote time outside of class to students, and engaged in the schools' religious mission.

- **Formation.** Schools normally require all teachers to attend Ignatian retreats or other mission-based education activities annually, with added formation activities for pretenure faculty. Forming for mission helps ensure that the Jesuit schools will retain their Ignatian character.
- **Communication.** JSEA provides numerous print and online resources to help schools learn what other Jesuit schools are doing and act accordingly.
- **Boards of Directors.** Jesuit high schools educate their board members about Ignatian spirituality and mission, because the boards set the tone for schools and are more successful in fundraising when they better understand the mission and vision.

As a result of this common spirituality and worldview, visiting a succession of Jesuit schools feels like visiting the same school in different cities. They are all intensely proud to be Jesuit. They use the same language, display the same symbols, and follow common operating principles. AMDG is ubiquitous. As Fr. Deye says, lay educators and Jesuits are now carrying the torch of Jesuit education together.

Outline of the Book

The book begins with vignettes to give readers the flavor of life in today's Jesuit high schools. Then it moves to an explanation of Ignatian spirituality that translates essential jargon. This second chapter includes a profile of Fr. Larry Gillick, SJ, director of Creighton University's Deglman Center for Ignatian Spirituality and an alum of Marquette University High School, who joined the Jesuits as a brother in the era when a blind man could not be ordained. Also included in the chapter is Fr. Gillick's beautiful meditation on discernment.

After this, I explore the impact of Ignatian ideals on the major facets of school life: academics, spiritual life, discipline, and student life, including cocurricular activities and athletics. If you ever spent a day in JUG, you'll love meeting two traditional Jesuit disciplinarians, Br. Douglas Draper, SJ, of St. Ignatius Prep in San Francisco, and Br. Casey Ferlita, SJ, of Strake Jesuit—I promise!

The next section portrays Jesuit high schools that serve special communities, including the Cristo Rey high schools; schools that anchor inner-city neighborhoods; Red Cloud High School, on South Dakota's Pine Ridge Reservation; and the "school within a school" that Houston's Strake Jesuit and New Orleans Jesuit created after Hurricane Katrina.

The chapters include profiles of the extraordinary people who make up the Jesuit high school family—faculty, students, and alums. Their lives exemplify Ignatian spirituality in contemporary American society. Finally, I provide brief profiles of ten outstanding alums from various schools, thumbnail sketches of all the Jesuit high schools, and a look at the future of Jesuit high school education.

Significance of Jesuit Schools

Jesuit education has survived because it is based on eternal verities and because it is life affirming and optimistic about discovering and teaching truth. It dreams great dreams and then finds ways to accomplish them. It instills accountability in adolescents who may not value this until later. It teaches high-potential youth the importance of serving others instead of living selfishly. As one of my favorite Creighton Prep alums says, "This form of education is nearly five hundred years old, its values are rock solid, and they have never been improved on."

Read these stories and reflect on your own life. What are you doing to change the world for the good? What might you do? Reconnect with Ignatian ideals if you've been exposed to them, or embrace them if they are new to you. Go forth and live as men and women for others in a world that desperately needs your gifts. Discover the joy that only serving God and others can bring!

PART I

JESUIT HIGH SCHOOLS

1

Scenes from Jesuit High Schools

The following vignettes from life at Jesuit high schools give a sense of who the people are, how they live, and what they value.

Preparing for Freshman Retreat

More than fifty Strake Jesuit College Preparatory students who would be leading the annual freshman retreat formed a silent circle on the darkened auditorium stage at a "pep rally" for the retreat. Elsewhere, the football team was preparing for the state play-offs. These young men would attend the game, but first things first.

"This retreat is so special," a student leader said. "We will instill a newfound love of God in the hearts of the freshmen. The freshmen don't know what to expect. We are called to be a light to the freshmen. Jesus said others will recognize us for our love. I've seen this, especially in the group leaders. You have all been witnesses of Christ."

In the background, a loudspeaker ordered members of the band to catch the bus to the play-off game. Several boys silently departed. The rest stood to embrace one another in a lengthy kiss of peace. No one rushed. Football could wait.

Meditation on the Hudson

Casually dressed Fordham Preparatory School faculty and staff took in a spectacular view of the Hudson River on a perfect fall morning at a retreat center. They were half an hour and a million miles away from the urban clamor of East Fordham Road in the Bronx.

"What is your image of God, and what attitudes in you does that foster?" asked retreat director Fr. Larry Gillick, SJ, of Creighton University. "What religious questions cause you the most tension that you would like to avoid?"

During thirty minutes of meditation, teachers strolled the hills, sat under trees sipping coffee, or lay on the ground contemplating God's will and the magnificent scenery, never breaking the silence. Fordham Prep requires faculty and staff to attend this retreat focused on discernment, and they love it.

"We look forward to this day all year long," said Paul Homer, a theology teacher and the director of the service program. "Seven years ago, we didn't know about this stuff. This is critical, because with fewer Jesuits, we are creating a culture and self-understanding that will carry on our Ignatian identity. Ignatius started with laypeople. There's no reason not to be optimistic that we can do this. The Jesuits recognize the power of the laity, and we share responsibility with the priests."

Burying the Dead

At St. Ignatius High School in Cleveland, the members of the St. Joseph of Arimathea Society have become trained pallbearers for people who die with no friends or relatives. "I think it's the most humbling thing I've ever done," says Brett Gigliotti, class of '06, a leader of the society who has served as a pallbearer at more than fifteen funerals. "What I realize from all these trips is that life is precious. I'm sure all these people we buried had stories to tell."

The service began in 2000, when St. Ignatius High's Christian Action Team looked for new ways to serve. "We thought, well, we have young guys who are strong and have time to donate," says James Skerl, a theology teacher.

Girls at St. Ignatius Prep

Lauren Totah and her father, Paul, have lunch during quarter exams at St. Ignatius Prep in San Francisco. She is a junior at the school. Her father is St. Ignatius Prep's director of public relations. Lauren comments that her physics test went well. Lauren is one of today's Jesuit high school "women for others."

Since 1983, when St. Ignatius Prep went coed, half its students have been females. "We went coed to keep our numbers up," says Paul Totah. "Our board was fifty-fifty on the idea. The alums said, 'You are crazy.' The Jesuits just said we would do it." Br. Douglas Draper, SJ, a longtime disciplinarian at the school, says coeducation has improved conduct at St. Ignatius Prep. "God made girls more mature at age fourteen. They bring the boys along. I think it's for the better."

Directing Operation Others

For more than twenty years, Creighton Prep theology teacher Bill Laird has directed Operation Others, an interschool program that feeds about fifteen hundred Omaha families every Christmas. He praises the students who spend months collecting money and food and then pack and deliver five thousand boxes of groceries. But the true heroes are the people who struggle in poverty every day. "I really hope we can find a better way to care for people who really need help," he says.

2

Ignatian Spirituality

If only there were a God Positioning System to help people discern the will of God! People would be a lot happier. They think discernment means eliminating the problem of uncertainty, but that's impossible if God is as St. Ignatius envisions him. Ignatian spirituality involves facing the religious questions that cause the most tension.

Fr. Larry Gillick, SJ, director,
Deglman Center for Ignatian Spirituality,
Creighton University

Ignatian spirituality is the engine that drives Jesuit high schools. It's an optimistic, demanding, world-engaging, loving vision of the relationship between God and God's people that leads Jesuit high schools to be simultaneously challenging and caring. It makes them schools that value their students individually and expect great things from them.

During formation, Jesuits absorb St. Ignatius's vision for his Society: to win the world for God by forming men and women for others. The lay educators who dominate today's Jesuit high schools enthusiastically collaborate in this mission, often with a fervor that amazes Jesuits. The motto of the Society of Jesus is *ad majorem Dei gloriam*, a Latin phrase meaning "for the greater glory of God." Shorthand for the motto is the acronym AMDG. This summarizes the high schools' spiritual quest: to do their best for God, whether it is organizing the best freshman retreat ever, winning the state swimming title, or having more National Merit finalists than any other school in the city.

Basic Premises of Ignatian Spirituality

St. Ignatius was a product of Spanish chivalry, so it's natural that his spirituality envisions a passionate romance between God and his world. Ignatius's holistic vision of the relationship between God and human beings can be summarized in these terms:

- It sees creation as a gift that calls forth wonder and gratitude.
- It gives scope to the imagination and to emotion as well as to the intellect.
- It seeks to find God in all things, including all people and cultures.
- It cultivates an awareness of personal and social evil but believes that God's love is more powerful than any evil.
- It stresses freedom, discernment, and responsible action.
- It empowers people to become leaders in service, building a more just and humane world.

Ignatian spirituality is joyful and optimistic. It sees the world and people as good because God made them. Jesuit schools celebrate scientific inquiry as a way to discover truths about God's creation. They encourage artistic expression because it encourages people to imaginatively explore their relationship with God. Jesuit schools find God in all things, even football.

St. Ignatius wanted to change the world for the good by changing the lives of people who would enlist in this glorious quest. Ever the practical soldier, he wrote *The Spiritual Exercises* as a training manual for his forces. This book has become perhaps the most influential spiritual manual of the last five hundred years. The principles it embodies drive Jesuit schools to mold high-potential students into leaders who will change the world for the good by serving others, especially the poor, and win the world for God.

The early Jesuits were controversial because they spent most of their time working among the people or teaching rather than withdrawing to a monastery to pray. Spiritual traditionalists saw them as too secular, and secularists saw them as too spiritual. Jesuits hear these same criticisms today. Over the centuries, Ignatius's followers have built on his insights and created a distinct attitude that we call "Ignatian spirituality." Unfortunately, Ignatian concepts are sometimes expressed in shoptalk that can seem obscure and intimidating. Here we will unpack these key Ignatian terms:

- The Spiritual Exercises
- Discernment
- *Magis*
- *Cura personalis*
- Finding God in all things
- Men and women for others

The Spiritual Dimension of Jesuit Education

The Society of Jesus' way of proceeding demands close collaboration with all "who hunger and thirst after justice" in order to make "a world where the brotherhood of all opens the way for the recognition and acceptance of Christ Jesus and God our Father." At the same time, the "Jesuit heritage of creative response to the call of the Spirit in concrete situations of life is an incentive to develop a culture of dialogue in our approach to believers of other religions." Therefore Jesuit schools "conscientize their students on the value of interreligious collaboration and instill in them a basic understanding of and respect for the faith vision of the members of the diverse local religious communities, while deepening their own response to God." The ultimate objective of the mission of education should be to contribute vitally to "the total and integral liberation of the human person leading to participation in the life of God himself."

—From *What Makes a Jesuit School Jesuit?*

The Spiritual Exercises

The Spiritual Exercises is the handbook for a renewed encounter with God that St. Ignatius of Loyola developed in the early decades of the sixteenth century. It is based on his own spiritual experiences and his experiences in guiding others. Every Jesuit goes through a monthlong retreat based on the Exercises at the beginning and the end of his training. The Exercises invite participants, guided by a spiritual director, to meditate on creation, sin, and forgiveness, as well as calling, ministry, and other aspects of Christian faith. Retreatants ponder the life, death, and resurrection of Jesus. The retreat makes use of the imagination; retreatants envision themselves participating in these events. They read Scripture passages and picture themselves at the scene; then they meditate on what this means in their lives. The goal of the Exercises is often discernment of the direction of one's life.

Jesuit schools encourage their lay teachers to make the Exercises or an abbreviated version of them and often offer such retreats as part of school ministry programs. Creighton University offers a version of the Exercises online at a site that averages more than a million hits a month (www.creighton.edu/collaborativeministry/online.html).

The Exercises are administered one-on-one to accommodate each person's concrete circumstances. Fr. Andy Alexander, SJ, of Creighton puts it this way: "A director gives the Spiritual Exercises one-on-one to an individual and becomes a mentor. In the Exercises, we have the framework. I send you away to reflect on the mystery of the Lord and ask you to pray on something personal. Then I ask you to reflect on what you received and what it means. This action-reflection process moved directly into Jesuit education."

Many of the signature traits of Ignatian schools are rooted in such understanding of the individual. These include extensive cocurricular mentoring, discipline based on personal accountability, and personal reflection in class assignments. Even though Jesuit high schools often have more than one thousand students and seldom assign mentors, few students fail to find a mentor or a niche, because Ignatian teachers instinctively reach out to students one-on-one in classes and activities.

Discernment

Discernment involves reflecting on potential life choices in the light of faith. What's best? What might God be trying to tell me? The concept grows from the Ignatian vision of a God who is active in our lives and in our decision making. Discernment requires listening, especially through prayer and silent reflection.

"Discernment is not a decision; it's a lifestyle. I think God has asked us to be appropriately human, to take in data in making decisions and to ask if this is in keeping with my relationship with God. I want to put myself in a position to be loved by God," said Fr. Gillick at the Fordham Prep retreat.

People often request assistance with discernment to eliminate the "problem of uncertainty," but faith journeys involve facing up to uncertainties, or God would not be God, he said. This is because "God will never give us anything that will make God obsolete. We would like a God to give us everything, but then we wouldn't need a God." People should see mystery as an invitation to become more attuned to the voice of God through prayer and contemplation.

Typically, Jesuit schools require an intense freshman retreat to immerse new students in Ignatian spirituality, and schools strongly encourage seniors to participate in a Kairos retreat before they graduate. There are other retreat opportunities in between. Ideally, the retreats teach Jesuit students how to discern—that is, how to listen to God.

A Meditation on Discernment

From a retreat for the Fordham Prep faculty conducted by Larry Gillick

If only there were a God Positioning System to help people discern the will of God! People would be a lot happier. They think discernment means eliminating the problem of uncertainty, but that's impossible if God is as St. Ignatius envisions him. Ignatian spirituality involves facing the religious questions that cause the most tension.

Ignatius is asking, Is there a God? What kind of God? At the heart of all of this is our image of God. If we are to understand Ignatian spirituality, God is active. God labors for us. If God is indolent, I have to do it all myself, or if God is an interested observer of us, we have to appease or schmooze him. Ignatius's image of God was that of a God who labors to give us ourselves.

People always want to know if God has a plan for their lives. Young people have the attitude that all I've got to do is figure it out or have someone tell me. People fear uncertainty and failure. But that too is not the Ignatian image of God.

In the history of the Jesuits, most of our ministries have been failures. It can't be the will of God to always be successful, because Jesus' earthly life was a failure. Faith is an adventure, but we want security. We want adventure, but we want road maps. We want both belts and suspenders. We want success.

In the Ignatian spiritual vision, people can't have both a faith journey and absolute certainty, because that would contradict God's role as God.

God will never give us anything that will make God obsolete. We would like a God to give us everything, but then we wouldn't need a God. God would be cruel if he said, I have a plan for you, and you have to figure it out.

Instead of viewing mystery as something to be solved, people should see it as an invitation to learn more. God is simple. We are the mystery. Jesus offers us the invitation to encounter all we are as human beings. Ignatian spirituality involves the embrace of this encounter. Discernment is based on a relationship with God, not a developing life strategy—and people don't like to operate this way.

Kids will come to my office and say, "Father, can we discern for ten minutes?" I go to my computer and type in God.com and their names and Social Security numbers. Students laugh and get the message. However, people have to struggle not to confuse what their ego is telling them with what God may be telling them.

What does God sound like? The problem is I'm very aware of what my ego sounds like. I like the sound of God sounding a lot like my ego.

Discernment is not a decision; it's a lifestyle. I think God has asked us to be appropriately human, to take in data in making decisions and to ask if this is in keeping with my relationship with God. I want to put myself in a position to be loved by God.

Discernment is the beginning, not the end, requiring the believer to watch what God does. Our decisions will never have such clarity as we would like. God's will is for us to make a decision that trusts God, making this an act of faith.

The Spiritual Exercises are about becoming so comfortable in who we are that we can listen to anyone. Our main problem is that we forget who we are.

Prayer is a way of God giving us our identity. Prayer is never narcissistic. Ignatian spirituality moves from contemplation to action, from prayer to the classroom or office. If you don't pray, you will forget who you are. You are sent in love and peace to serve others. If you are interested in staying focused and peaceful, are you important to you? We need to recover our identity by taking time for who we are.

The more you receive of yourself, the more you can give to others. What is Jesus giving me now?

Magis

Magis is Latin for "more." It's a shorthand term for the Jesuit commitment to excellence in everything. Students and teachers who aren't willing to give themselves to others should go elsewhere.

Like their soldier founder, early Jesuits sought victory in God's cause by giving "more than total commitment" and going "further than wholehearted service." Chris Lowney writes in *Heroic Leadership* that the "simple motto captures a broader spirit, a restless drive to imagine whether there isn't some even greater project to be accomplished or some better way of attacking the current problem."

Magis motivates everyone connected with Jesuit education to focus on mission, to contribute to the success of the enterprise, and to become a leader. Jesuit educators look for opportunities and solve problems. Says Lowney, "*Magis*-driven leadership inevitably leads to heroism. Heroism begins with each person considering, internalizing, and shaping his or her mission. . . . A *magis*-driven leader is not content to go through the motions or settle for the status quo but is restlessly inclined to look for something more, something greater. . . . Instead of waiting for golden opportunities, they find the gold in the opportunities at hand."

Ignatian educators frequently describe *magis* as the basis for their dedication and success. *Magis* contributes to the spirit that every Jesuit school I visited displayed in abundance.

Cura Personalis

Cura personalis is a Latin phrase meaning "care for the person." It is a hallmark of Ignatian spirituality and central to the Jesuit educational philosophy. It stems from respect for the dignity of human beings as unique creations of God and for "God's embracing of humanity in the person of Jesus," as described in *Do You Speak Ignatian?* Jesuits seek to lead and to manage more through love than through fear, working with passion and courage whether teaching teenagers or confronting the powerful who abuse the poor. In the classroom, *cura personalis* inspires teachers to listen to students, to build relationships with them, and to guide them in taking responsibility for their learning.

Cura personalis underlies the spirit of community at Jesuit schools. As Lowney writes, "Everyone knows that organizations, armies, sports teams, and companies perform best when team members respect, value, and trust one another and sacrifice narrow self-interest to support team goals. . . . Individuals perform best when they are respected, valued, and trusted by someone who genuinely cares for their well-being."

The accountability and the discipline at Jesuit schools manifest *cura personalis*. If teachers didn't love their students, they wouldn't make the extra effort that holding people accountable entails.

Magis and *cura personalis* are the yin and yang of Ignatian spirituality, balancing a creative tension between striving and supporting.

Finding God in All Things

Jesuit high schools find God everywhere, from campus chapels to chemistry labs. They view God at work in retreats and at basketball practices. Every aspect of school life offers opportunities for students to encounter God at work in their communities.

If this sounds like sanctifying what students enjoy or must endure, Ignatius would probably beg to differ. He viewed the universe as "proceeding from God and returning to God, linking the ongoing creation to its consummation," says Ronald Modras in his book *Ignatian Humanism*. Consequently, Ignatian spirituality "invites a person to search for and find God in every circumstance of life, not just in explicitly religious situations or activities. It implies that God is present everywhere and, though invisible, can be 'found' in any and all of the creatures which God has made" (*Do You Speak Ignatian?*).

Finding a relationship with God in all things requires the believer to be attentive and reverent, becoming alert to what is "really there," whether he or she is focusing on a person, a poem, a social injustice, or a scientific experiment. The goal is to determine the way that God is working in a particular situation. As Modras writes, "If Ignatian spirituality seeks and finds 'God in all things,' it is because everything is grace."

Profile: Fr. Larry Gillick, SJ
A Blind Man Who Helps Others See

Fr. Larry Gillick joined the Jesuits as a brother in 1960 knowing that he couldn't become a priest because he had been blinded in a childhood accident. Before Vatican II, the church would not ordain a blind man. Gillick spent his first five years as a Jesuit working in a laundry or as a janitor because brothers were banned from further education and professional careers within the Society. He never resented this, because "we almost gloried in the humility of it." However, God had different plans for him. After Vatican II, Gillick not only was ordained but also became a noted spiritual director and retreat leader.

Gillick credits his family and the Jesuits for helping him overcome the barrier of blindness. His mother never coddled him or allowed him to accept standard restrictions on the blind. Like the rest of his family, Gillick attended Marquette University High School, instead of a school for the visually impaired. His mother read him his assignments. He was a member of the homecoming court.

Marquette University High fostered Gillick's vocation. "I've always been fascinated by importance. I always wondered who was important and why. My grandfather was an alderman, and my father was a lawyer. I had met politicians and judges and lawyers, but I figured out that the Jesuits had a sense of their importance. It's an important game when men would give their lives serving others."

Fr. Bill Neenan, SJ, of Boston College, then a seminarian, was a strong influence. "He taught us fourth-year Latin, but if we did five days of Latin in four days we would spend Fridays on social issues such as unions, just wages, and integration. This was Milwaukee in 1957–58, and all that was kind of new to us. Those were wonderful classes, more interesting than Virgil." Neenan later assisted at Gillick's first Mass.

Gillick attended St. Norbert College, in Wisconsin, for two years before entering the Jesuit brotherhood. While at college, he dated, was equipment manager of the football team, and was a class officer. After joining the Jesuits, he uncomplainingly accepted limitations that included living, eating, and even praying separately from the priests and the Scholastics. "I never felt denigrated."

When the ban on ordaining men with disabilities was abolished, Gillick's superiors urged him to study for the priesthood. About fifty people supported his petition to superior general Pedro Arrupe. Arrupe changed Gillick's status, permitting him to be ordained in 1972, along with a number of his Marquette University High classmates. "The Jesuits saw more in me than I saw in myself," he says. Years later, Gillick met Arrupe in an infirmary in Rome after Arrupe had suffered a debilitating stroke. Gillick asked if the superior remembered him. "All those letters," replied Arrupe in Spanish, the only language he could still speak.

Gillick's career has included several assignments at Jesuit high schools, and he usually conducts several retreats a year for the faculties of various schools. His wisdom and gentle humor make him an instant hit with his audiences; he translates the complexities of Ignatian spirituality into concrete terms that teachers can apply in their own lives and convey to students.

"Fr. Gillick is fantastic," says Paul Homer, a theology teacher at Fordham Preparatory School who attended one of Gillick's retreats. "He has a wonderful way. His insights are challenging." Faculty retreats are a major way of strengthening the Ignatian identity of Jesuit high schools even as their Jesuit presence shrinks.

Fr. Larry Gillick may be blind, but he has helped countless people see.

Men and Women for Others

This modern cornerstone of Jesuit education dates to 1973, when Fr. Pedro Arrupe, SJ, called for a reeducation in justice, stating that "today our prime educational objective must be to form men and women for others; . . . men and women who cannot even conceive of love of God which does not include love for the least of their neighbors; men and women completely convinced that love of God which does not issue in justice for others is a farce" (*Do You Speak Ignatian?*). At their Thirty-Fourth General Council, the Jesuits called on members to be not only "men for others" but also "men with others."

Today's Jesuit high schools have taken Arrupe's mandate to heart. Schools such as Red Cloud High School, on the Pine Ridge Reservation, and the Cristo Rey schools educate economically disadvantaged students. Tuition-free Regis High School, in New York, sponsors an intensive tutoring program to prepare low-income students to compete for admission. Many high schools assist local Jesuit Nativity middle schools that have the mission of preparing low-income students to succeed in high school.

National Jesuit standards, as outlined in *What Makes a Jesuit School Jesuit?* admonish all Jesuit schools to

- Maintain a clear sense of justice and respect for the legitimate rights of others in their dealings with all constituencies: "The entire institution not only teaches justice but also acts justly"
- Manifest "solidarity with the poor by offering generous amounts of financial aid based on need" and by recruiting and retaining students from families of "limited means"
- Offer "effective Christian service programs which enable students to serve people in need thoughtfully and reflectively"

Arrupe's vision is alive and growing throughout the United States. It seems particularly fitting that the Cristo Rey high school in Denver is named after him.

Men for Others in Houston

At Houston's Strake Jesuit College Preparatory, seniors must perform one hundred hours of community service before they graduate, but most do more. Four members of the class of '06 described how their service had influenced their lives.

Jimmy McLean spent 196 hours as a counselor at a camp for children with epilepsy. He said that he hopes to return to the camp, where he worked as a staff member.

Trey McBee had a "so-so attitude" when he began working as a camp counselor for disabled children. However, "five hours into it, I was having lots of fun." He contributed 143 hours of service.

Sean Caine, who also served as a camp counselor, loved working with children so much that he plans to major in elementary education. "If it weren't for the service requirement, I probably wouldn't have found this out. I want to do more and more. At first it seemed like a week out of my summer, but then I wished it had been longer." He also "put in lots of hours" helping to fix up homes for the poor.

Chris Zubaneh, a soccer player of Palestinian descent, spent three weeks in Jerusalem running a soccer camp for poor Palestinian and Israeli children. "The Palestinian kids didn't have anything—no training gear. The facilities were a concrete field. I brought the balls. It was really rewarding to help them learn the game. The [Palestinian] kids were friends with the Israelis. It was a really rewarding experience."

Strake Jesuit emphasizes the "men for others" mantra. McLean recalled the day the water polo team encountered a young woman with a flat tire. "The coach asked, 'Who wants to be a man for others?' Three people helped change the tire, even though it delayed them twenty-five minutes."

3

Academic Excellence

....

We have the most National Merit Scholars of any school.

> Ian Gunn, class of '07,
> Jesuit High School, New Orleans

We've had tremendous press in the Indianapolis media. A magazine has ranked Brebeuf the top school in the city.

> Sarah Steele, class of '93, admissions director,
> Brebeuf Jesuit Preparatory School

In Portland, as in many cities, Jesuit seems to be the preeminent school in town.

> Paul Hogan, academic vice principal,
> Jesuit High School, Portland, Oregon

Whether it is Red Cloud High School, on South Dakota's Pine Ridge Reservation, or Regis High School in Manhattan, Jesuit high schools consider themselves the toughest academic game in town. They boast of their SAT/ACT scores, their number of National Merit finalists, and their graduates admitted to elite universities. Academic stars often have almost as much status as top athletes. Most schools can claim at least a few alums who are Academy Award winners, pro athletes, top government officials, or famous authors.

There's irony in this. Although a Jesuit high school diploma is one of the nation's better passports to academic success, the schools view such success as merely a means to an end, not an end in itself. Jesuit schools are driven by the vision of Ignatius that they exist to save souls and prepare students to change the world for the good. The purpose of these institutions is not to populate the nation's medical and law schools.

Timothy Hanchin, a theology teacher at Boston College High School, argues that without a central focus on the life of St. Ignatius and the "countercultural character" of Jesuit education, "a great miseducation can occur," making Jesuit schools "indistinguishable from other elite college preparatory schools." Dr. Bernard Bouillette, vice president of the Jesuit Secondary Education Association (JSEA), says, "What makes a school really good is how it is living its mission."

The distinctive pedagogical style of Jesuit high schools is grounded in *The Spiritual Exercises*'s assumption that studying, analyzing, embracing, and interpreting God's world is a way to understand God. Jesuit schools value scientific inquiry and artistic expression. Students and teachers become companions on the journey to God.

"Ignatius placed incredible value on the gifts that God gives us, including our brains," says Mary Abinante, a campus ministry staff member at St. Ignatius Prep in San Francisco. "Part of finding God is not being afraid of anything, because God is there. We embrace the best that can be found in any discipline. It is not an accident that the Jesuits run prestigious academic institutions."

Ignatian pedagogy goes beyond academic mastery. It is concerned with "students' well-rounded growth as persons for others" (*Do You Speak Ignatian?*). Ignatian teachers are expected to regularly engage in "comprehensive assessment" of their students' growth and their "generosity in response to common needs," says Fr. Ralph Metts, SJ, in *Ignatius Knew*.

Ignatian Pedagogy in Action

Like most other Jesuit schools, Portland Jesuit High uses the Ignatian pedagogical paradigm (IPP), which is based on integrating context, experience, reflection, action, and evaluation. Academic vice principal Paul Hogan says, "The paradigm is about asking hard questions and integrating new knowledge into old. How does this expand your worldview? Jesuit teachers begin by asking themselves, What is the readiness of my students, and what is going on in their lives? You have to know these."

Hogan says that his British literature unit on Jonathan Swift's eighteenth-century satire *A Modest Proposal* illustrates the IPP in action. In *A Modest Proposal*, Swift suggests that impoverished Irish families earn money by fattening up their starving babies and selling them to rich landowners to be eaten. Hogan opens the unit by focusing on *context* and *experience*—how much do the students already know about the conditions of people in eighteenth-century Ireland? Do they understand satire?

Next, students move to *reflection*. They might journal to discern the broader implications of this work for Swift's society and ours. Do they understand that this piece is about poverty and homelessness in all eras? This is followed by *action*. "In this class, we do a homeless immersion," says Hogan. "We might spend a day hanging out with the homeless in Portland, then writing letters to the paper or the governor. Students are likely to have their horizons broadened." Finally, the students do an *evaluation* of the material and their experiences.

Discovering a Sacred World

Quotes from a meditation on the impact of the Spiritual Exercises on Jesuit education, by Fr. John J. Callahan, SJ

The principle of *magis*. "Ignatius asks that a person not even consider choosing the second-rate. His challenge: freely choose the 'more.'"

The goodness of the world. "Everything that exists comes from and reveals a loving, creating God. Therefore, everything is open for study and inquiry. In principle, there cannot be a contradiction between science and religion. . . . The more one knows about the universe, the more one knows about God."

Hope in the presence of evil. "To participate in creating the world, one must know it well and be able to subject everything to a rigorous critique. Values, too, must be based on the God-given desire to create a loving world."

The importance of the imagination. "Through imagination a person can see, taste, hear, and feel God's desires and the beauty of creation. . . . Imagination is the initial step in a person's participating in God's creative power."

The teacher as companion. Jesuit education emphasizes the experiences of the student, not those of the teacher (a reflection of the emphasis on the retreatant in the Exercises). "To instruct is essential to being a teacher. To listen, to build on student experiences and insights, to support, and to gently guide are even more so."

Focus on Students

Ignatian education focuses on helping students integrate knowledge into their lives, not just memorize facts. Jesuit schools emphasize teacher-student relationships, because the Spiritual Exercises stress the relationship between director and retreatant. Teachers are guides to understanding, not just dispensers of facts.

Jesuit schools rarely assign mentors, because "students find their own mentors," Hogan says. Students must believe that their teachers care about them, because "the number one determinant of whether students learn is whether they believe that the teacher likes them." Teachers must greet students by name and know them well enough to ask questions about their activities and their lives.

"Our former president used to say that no student should go through Jesuit without several adults knowing them well and caring deeply," says Hogan. There's nothing soft about such caring. Jesuit schools attract both teachers and students who are goal-driven and like the emphasis on rigor, achievement, and accountability. Highly motivated teachers are allowed to innovate as they push students as far as possible. Jesuit schools stress clear expectations and accountability more than personal freedom and flexibility.

Regis High School

Regis High School graduate Matt McGough served two seasons as a batboy for the New York Yankees while he was in high school. In *Bat Boy*, he relates his experience at Regis.

> As an all-scholarship school, Regis is private but tuition-free. . . . In return, the school expects a great deal from its students; like most of its graduates, I found everything after high school— college, graduate school—comparatively a breeze. If you failed a class at Regis, you were required to make up that work in a monthlong, five-morning-a-week summer session. If you failed in the summer session to satisfy the school's requirements, you were forced to relinquish your scholarship which meant finding another high school to attend. . . . Failing summer school would

mean leaving a school I loved. . . . I'd have to lower my hopes and expectations as to the colleges that I might attend. I'd be cut off from all my friends at Regis, the only close friends I felt I had since leaving my neighborhood middle school for a high school in the City.

Regis has always been a special Jesuit high school because it has never charged tuition. Originally this enabled poor immigrants to receive a Jesuit education, but gradually students became more and more middle-class and upper-middle-class. Regis found that few low-income students could meet its extremely rigorous admissions standards. To change this, it created REACH (Recruiting Excellence in Academics for Catholic High Schools), an intensive tutoring program.

Most of the first students enrolled in the program attended impoverished inner-city Catholic elementary schools. Their parents were blue-collar workers—hospital personnel, teacher's aides, restaurant workers, and cab drivers—who came to the United States from Africa, India, Bangladesh, Poland, and Ireland. In fifth grade, these students tested at the eightieth percentile—far too low to be admitted to selective New York Jesuit high schools.

Three years later, after completing Regis High School's REACH program, this group of thirty boys tested at the ninety-sixth percentile and won two million dollars in scholarships to private high schools, mostly Jesuit. A third of them were admitted to Regis. After their first trimester at Regis, alums of the REACH program had grades that "were solid and improving," says Fr. Christopher Devron, SJ, director of the program. In addition, they were class leaders in theater, basketball, and student government.

REACH participants take weekend enrichment courses in math, language arts, and study skills and spend three weeks one summer at the University of Scranton to get exposure to college. REACH also emphasizes the growth of faith and leadership through prayer, retreats, reflection, and community service. Unlike most Jesuit high schools, Regis accepts only Catholics.

The school is noted for sending graduates to elite colleges. Regis's alumni roster reads like a Who's Who of lawyers, judges, doctors, clergy, educators, business leaders, and noted authors, such as Edward Conlon, who wrote *Blue Blood*, describing life as a Harvard-educated New York cop.

Regis is not an athletic powerhouse, but distinguished alums include three *Sports Illustrated* staff members (senior editor Larry Burke and writers Daniel Habib and Pete McEntegart) and Gene Orza, chief operating officer of the Major League Baseball Players Association.

Chris Lowney, class of '76, is the author of *Heroic Leadership*, a book exploring Jesuit leadership. Lowney says his experience at Regis changed his life "in every way. My best friends are from my freshman class. My faith was largely steeled by what I learned there. The place opened up all kinds of possibilities in terms of learning and career."

However, Lowney challenges all Jesuit schools to assess the results of their "exemplary service programs" by imagining "what a 'woman for others' looks like twenty years from graduation," determining a "threshold percentage of any class that would be considered a good result at developing men and women for others," and then figuring out how many are actually doing this. If the schools don't do such assessment, the phrase *men and women for others* "can just run into well-meaning but nonrigorous rhetoric."

The Curricula

The curricula of American Jesuit high schools are rooted in the *Ratio Studiorum*, the original Jesuit plan of studies, which emphasized the liberal arts, math, science, and language. Strong core requirements are key to students' academic success. Jesuit alums often salute their schools for preparing them well, especially in writing. A typical Jesuit high school graduate will complete a minimum of

- Four years each of theology and English
- Three years each of science, math, and history/social science
- Two years of a foreign language, with 85 percent taking three or four years
- One year of fine arts

Many schools require their students to develop technology skills, and most schools integrate social justice activities with some academic courses. Jesuit schools usually offer fewer electives than public schools but often supplement the core with special offerings to meet the needs of their students. For example, Red Cloud High School has a Lakota studies program. Loyola High School in Detroit, which enrolls some two hundred inner-city African American boys, helps its at-risk students overcome their academic deficits. New York's Xavier High School was originally a Jesuit military school and still sponsors a Junior ROTC program and a nationally ranked drill team. Gonzaga College High School, in Washington, DC, sends its freshman theology classes to the Holocaust Museum, its art classes to the National Gallery, its English students to the Folger Shakespeare Library, and its science classes to the Smithsonian. St. Xavier High School in Cincinnati compensates for its relatively large size (fifteen hundred students) by assigning freshmen to "houses" of about seventy-five students who have the same English, theology, and world cultures teachers. These students also attend retreats, take field trips, and socialize together. Seattle Preparatory School collaborates with Seattle University in the award-winning Matteo Ricci College program, which allows students to receive a high school diploma and a BA in six years.

Jesuit students everywhere study hard. Typical homework loads are ninety minutes to three hours a day, but students invest massive amounts of time in order to excel in cocurricular activities such as Academic Decathlon, debate, forensics, student publications, and science competitions. Rockhurst High School, in Kansas City, Missouri, boasts one of the nation's top high school journalism programs. Creighton Prep consistently ranks in the top schools in its division in the national Academic Decathlon.

"In a Jesuit high school, the top students have the same status as athletes. Often they are the same students," Hogan says. "In a Jesuit school, it's cool to be really smart. Everyone has to be a geek on some level." Students who win academic competitions are honored at pep rallies, just as athletes are. Portland Jesuit, for example, simultaneously honored both the state champion boys swim team and the Science Bowl team, who had won the northwest regional.

Unfortunately, the Jesuit reputation for academic rigor deters some students from even applying to the schools. Although all Jesuit schools have entrance exams and a significant number have competitive admissions, many accept students with a range of academic skills.

"Parents will tell me, 'My Jimmy would never make it at Jesuit,'" says Hogan. "But we want to help regular students get ready for college. A lot of our most loyal alums had 2.0 grade point averages but got the skills to succeed. More schools are taking more risks with poor kids from the local Nativity middle schools. I've told a number of students that the 4.0 students are easy, but they aren't the ones who make our jobs as fulfilling as regular kids who finally get it."

St. Ignatius Prep, San Francisco

It was quarter exams week at St. Ignatius Prep, in a neighborhood of San Francisco. Its 1,415 students moved to and from their tests with the purposefulness of those paying more than thirteen thousand dollars a year in tuition to attend a school that accepts only about a fourth of its applicants. A fifth of those who attend the school receive financial aid. The privilege of attending St. Ignatius Prep carries a future price tag as well. Students know that they will be expected to give back to society, especially to the poor.

"We are involved in a great conspiracy to put intellectually competent young men and women into society with a lifetime vision to serve others," says Charlie Dullea, class of '65, principal since 1997. This school is Ignatian to the core.

"AMDG is infused in this building," says English teacher Elizabeth Purcell. St. Ignatius Prep requires all faculty members to participate in one Ignatian evening a year that includes a liturgy and a presentation on an Ignatian theme. Campus ministry and the adult spirituality office sponsor prayer groups, Advent and Lenten series, and numerous retreats. "The better adults are spiritually, the better teachers they will become," says Dullea.

Like other Jesuit high schools, St. Ignatius Prep has experienced massive changes since its teachers attended the school. When Dullea and math teacher Chuck Murphy, class of '61, were students at St. Ignatius Prep, it was all-male, and the teachers were mostly Jesuits. Today, it is coed, and there are only a handful of Jesuits.

Because of St. Ignatius Prep's proximity to Berkeley and Haight-Ashbury, the cultural upheavals of the 1960s and '70s hit the school particularly hard. Murphy recalls those tempestuous years and laments that "things got too loose" for a while.

"When I [became a teacher] here in 1966, two kids were kicked out two weeks before graduation for smoking marijuana," says Murphy, whose father also was a longtime St. Ignatius Prep teacher. "Within three years, we had a policy that the users could stay, and the pushers had to go."

In 1973, "people wore armbands because a popular priest was not named academic vice principal," he says. On another occasion, Scholastics who had been studying at the Jesuit School of Theology at Berkeley "stood up in faculty town-hall meetings and told the principal to resign because he wasn't allowing the faculty to express itself." Some popular Jesuits left both St. Ignatius Prep and the Society.

St. Ignatius Prep survived and now is thriving spiritually, academically, and financially. "I think the future is really bright," Dullea says. "The Jesuits trained us well. Now we have to educate our lay faculty. The emphasis has to be on contemplation in action. We have to have reflection and action."

Faculty Snapshots

Katie Wolf, Fine Arts. Fine arts chair Katie Wolf created the school's art curriculum and designed its elegant Jensen Chapel. When she arrived in 1973, there were no art courses. Now all students must take a year of fine arts. "I want students to sense that they are creators in the same sense that their Creator has created all of us—that we mirror each other and the face of God." Wolf teaches a "sacred symbols" course that examines the way art, architecture, and religious imagery convey messages about cultures, religions, and the arts. The course also fulfills a senior religion elective requirement. "When you are involved with the creative process, you follow an educational circle. It is natural to create an expression, reflect on it, and change it."

Elizabeth Purcell, English. Elizabeth Purcell believes that she can instill ideals like the preferential option for the poor through teaching literature. That's why she quit a high-paying educational consultant job in Washington, DC, to return to teaching. "I am passionate about teaching. The years I was a consultant, I made a lot of money. Consulting allowed me to make a lot of money for people who had money, but it did nothing for my heart. Teaching allows my heart to sing. I tell the kids that I don't like grown-ups."

Purcell sees her literature classes as religious-studies courses. "For example, when I teach *Native Son*, I love to talk about racial injustice. That's also true of *Huck Finn*. Every piece of literature allows us to do that."

Chuck Murphy, Math. Chuck Murphy believes that St. Ignatius Prep is "more Jesuit than when I graduated in 1961. There's more emphasis on service now than then. Your faith is important. I believe in men and women for others." The "colleagueship" that Murphy has shared with his Jesuit and lay associates explains much of his devotion to St. Ignatius Prep. He treasures memories of retreats, home Masses, and friendships with fellow faculty members. Murphy's father, J. B. Murphy, served as a teacher, a coach, and an athletic director at St. Ignatius Prep from 1939 to 1989 and became known as "Mr. SI." He was noted for knowing everything about every student and frequently going to boys' homes to help with family problems in the era before counselors.

Fr. John Becker, SJ, English. Becker taught English at St. Ignatius between 1958 and 1978 and also moderated the newspaper, inspiring alums such as Peter Casey (cocreator of TV's *Frasier*) to become professional writers. "He was tough. He could nail you if you weren't paying attention, but he never did it in a malicious way," says Casey. "When he told me that I could write, it made an impression on me. That praise helped steer me to major in journalism at a junior college and in broadcasting when I transferred to San Francisco State University."

College Counseling

Jesuit high schools expect all their students to go to college, and the schools emphasize college counseling. Rockhurst High School provides an example of how these systems work.

Rich Sullivan, a college counselor, says that sophomores tour the college counseling office to discuss what they are looking for in a college. That spring, they take the PSAT. In junior year, students take the SAT and/or the ACT and attend a college information night with their parents that exposes them to Jesuit, Catholic, and highly selective colleges. Students reflect on themselves and their choices. The school encourages students to visit colleges.

"Hopefully, by September of their senior year they have done some of these things," says Sullivan. "We like for them to have their applications in by Christmas. We do the counselor recommendations and the teacher recommendations." Sullivan says that when he writes a recommendation, he tries to include helpful insights into the student.

In May, Rockhurst holds a college fair that draws one hundred colleges. It also cosponsors a financial aid night with its all-female sister schools, St. Teresa's Academy and Notre Dame de Sion High School, and provides an extensive financial aid Web site. In a typical year, more than one hundred colleges and universities nationwide accept Rockhurst students.

"We want to give them options," says Sullivan. "This is really about helping them discern. We try to get them to put something on their lists that they hadn't thought about. We do a lot of informal advising."

De Smet and Judge Autrey

If Henry Autrey had attended his local public high school, it's unlikely he would be sitting on the federal district court in St. Louis. Judge Autrey, an African American from a poor family, would likely have been channeled into the slow math classes and the manual education (vocational) track because of his poor standardized scores. Fortunately, his Catholic school eighth-grade teacher steered him to De Smet, the new Jesuit high school just opening near his home, because he was an excellent student.

At De Smet, Autrey excelled in both academics and football. He played offense as well as defense but preferred defense, because it "allows you to take out your aggressions."

His favorite subject was Spanish, which led him to a course in Latin American politics. This stimulated his interest in American government, politics, and law. He majored in political science at St. Louis University and received a scholarship from SLU's School of Law. He was a prosecuting trial attorney and then a local judge before being appointed a federal judge in 2002.

Autrey boasts two De Smet "firsts." Because his last name begins with *A*, he was the first graduate in the school's first graduating class. Later, he was elected the first member of De Smet's Hall of Fame.

"If I hadn't gone to De Smet, I can guarantee that I wouldn't be [serving as a judge]," he says.

Autrey credits De Smet with giving him the one-on-one attention that stimulated his intellectual growth. "They won't let you slide through. They work hard at keeping you. You have to work hard to reciprocate." Being rich or poor made no difference. Rich kids who were lazy "didn't stay in. They couldn't cut the mustard."

He hopes that his son will attend De Smet. "It made a night-and-day difference in my life."

A College Perspective

Donald Bishop, associate vice president for enrollment management at Creighton University, explains why a senior in the top third of a Jesuit high school class is usually as attractive to selective colleges as a student in the top 10 percent of other good high schools. A typical SAT score for Jesuit high school seniors is 1250–1350, which translates to the top 10 to 15 percent. The national average is 1020. A typical ACT score for Jesuit high school students is 25–29 (which translates to about the same percentages), while the national average is 21.

"This means that the median kid at a Jesuit high school is in the top 15 to 20 percent of the nation. When selective colleges are looking at class rank, we rate the high school's quality and adjust for it. Jesuit kids have taken stronger courses and more classes. Jesuit high school graduates typically have completed twenty or more one-year units in core subjects, versus sixteen to eighteen at most schools. We see more internal rigor in those courses. It is a reason for the higher SAT and ACT scores."

Numerous Jesuit high school Web sites boast that their school has more National Merit semifinalists than other schools in their area, and nearly all Jesuit high schools proclaim that 97 percent or more of their graduates go to college.

St. Ignatius College Prep, Chicago

Latin and classical Greek thrive at St. Ignatius College Prep in Chicago. The school is nationally known for its classics curriculum. St. Ignatius has always offered two years of Greek and four of Latin. However, during the 1960s, enrollment in the classics slipped, says Frank Raispis, class of '45, who has taught at St. Ignatius since 1955.

His response was to create a Greek-Latin course open only to the top incoming freshmen. The principal, a "fan of the classics," agreed to lengthen the class by half a period at the beginning of the day. The course became a St. Ignatius institution.

In the first year of the combination class, "I got about twenty kids," Raispis says. "This year, I have forty-four kids taking Greek-Latin in two sections. Interest is expanding." The classes are demanding. Freshmen read sixteen hundred lines of Homer. "We stress the language."

Classics students get excited about the "age-old appeal of discussions on the wellsprings of Western civilization," he says. "Language, art, and architecture are Greek and Roman." In addition, the classics are "the heart of Jesuit education," because they "make students more aware of who they are as people." The ancient Greek epics are stories of human beings on a journey—with all their strengths and foibles.

"We transfer this to a Catholic environment," says Raispis. "If the Incarnation is what we say it is, God became human. Why? The best way to find God in all things is to do it through the stories of humans—Romans and Greeks."

Teaching Young Men

Most Jesuit high schools are still all-male, at a time when the academic problems of boys are drawing increasing national concern. Eighty percent of high school dropouts are boys. Boys are, on average, a year to a year and a half behind girls in reading and writing skills. Boys get the majority of Ds and Fs in most schools and constitute 80 percent of the discipline problems. Young men make up less than 44 percent of the college population.

Why do Jesuit schools succeed in teaching boys when others are failing?

John Weetenkamp, director of Ignatian mission and identity at all-male Loyola Blakefield, in Towson, Maryland, points to Ignatian pedagogy. It emphasizes *action*, not just sitting in class and listening to lectures. Teachers integrate hands-on activities into learning and use a coaching style of teaching that boys enjoy. Social factors also promote success. Jesuit schools provide strong role models in the classroom, and most of the teachers also supervise cocurricular activities. They become mentors. A high percentage of these teachers are male—70 percent at Loyola Blakefield. In addition, most students come from families who value excellence, resulting in both a competitive atmosphere and peer pressure to do well.

Alums Critique Their Education

Portland Jesuit, a coed school with 1,140 students, surveys its graduates to assess their success in college and their satisfaction with their college preparation.

Here are examples of what they have said:

- "Overall I felt that JHS prepared me *very* well for college. I was amazed at how much greater my writing skills are compared to others'."

- "Jesuit put me in the front of the freshman pack at the University of Oregon when it comes to writing level. Papers are a cinch, and I have even started my own business, charging people a lunch or dinner at the dorms to edit their papers."

- "Jesuit needs to have more lecture-intense classes if it wants to truly be a college preparatory school, because I had few classes that had real lectures, and that was a huge shock for me when I got to college. I felt unprepared to handle that from the experiences I had at Jesuit."

- "I feel very prepared for college thanks to Jesuit. I know how to manage my time and keep up with my assignments."

Most alums are particularly grateful for their strong preparation in writing, although there are scattered complaints about other programs and departments. One alum's remarks capture the overall impact of the alum's high school experience: "At Jesuit, teachers want you to come to them with questions or if you need help. Knowing that teachers were eager to help at Jesuit helped me approach professors at college. Jesuit was a great experience. I feel lucky to have been able to go there and will always treasure my experiences there—both inside and outside the classroom."

4

Spiritual Life

....

AMDG is infused in this building.

Elizabeth Purcell,

St. Ignatius Prep, San Francisco

At a lake north of San Francisco, a dozen students from St. Ignatius Prep sit around a campfire praying after a night wilderness hike. "You have an immediate sense of peace and being in the hand of God," says fine arts chair Katie Wolf, who developed this retreat to help students "embrace God's creation."

At Seattle Prep, a "God Squad" of nine freshmen, three dads, and one Jesuit toured Jesuit missions and historical sites throughout Montana, Idaho, and Washington after spending a year sharing their faith and having fun together. "Our trip was about building up both faith and friendship, and by having the trip focus on both of those ideals, we were able to grow in both as well," says God Squad member Marc Snedden. "By learning about Jesuit history and meeting Jesuits, we were able to learn not only about Jesuit spirituality but our own as well."

At Red Cloud High School, the basketball team prays in a student-built Lakota sweat lodge several times a season, says coach Matt Rama. The lodge resembles a sauna in a ten-foot-wide enclosed circular tent. The Lakota find God in all things just as St. Ignatius did, says Tina Merdanian, class of '90, public relations director.

Spiritual Development

Guided by Ignatian tradition, Jesuit high schools invite students to find God through community service, pop music and culture, fine arts, travel, outdoor activities, and ethnic celebrations in addition to traditional liturgy. Ignatius believed that prayer should involve the senses and the entire person and promoted the interplay of experience, reflection, and action.

Schools surround students with powerful images of Christ, the saints, and Ignatian messages. *AMDG* appears in wall mosaics and on floor tiles. Crucifixes hang on the walls in most classrooms. Next to signs urging the football team to take state are posters announcing spiritual activities. Get involved with God, they proclaim. Join a religious rock group. Sign up for a summer service trip. Come to a Fellowship of Christian Athletes meeting.

Fr. Larry Gillick, SJ, says that Jesuit high schools resemble the inn in the parable of the Good Samaritan. They welcome young people with all their fears and injuries and take care of them because that is what Jesus did. The schools say to the students, "I want to give you yourself." This is the nature of God's love and of Jesus. "I want to give you 'you,' not make you something you are not."

The three stages of spiritual development in high schools are spiritual awareness, self-acceptance, and donation.

First is **spiritual awareness**. Many students select their Jesuit high schools for academic or athletic excellence rather than spirituality, but they become more spiritually aware during their time there. A Jesuit proverb summarizes this outcome: the students "enter by their door and leave by ours." Ignatian educators integrate spiritual development into every aspect of high school life.

In class, students reflect on the relationship between what they are learning and what they value. They journal about the moral themes implicit in what they are reading and doing. Cocurricular and extra-curricular activities and programs reinforce reflection, awareness, and accountability. A coach might ask a player to reflect on what life lessons she's learned from skipping practice and letting God, herself, and the team down. Students doing community service in impoverished areas might discuss their reactions to the poor. Some schools involve parents. Creighton Prep, for example, teaches parents of freshmen at a manda-tory "theology night" how to talk with their reluctant teens about sex, drugs and alcohol, and other life issues.

As students become more self-aware and aware that God loves them, they move to the next stage, **self-acceptance**, Gillick says. Self-acceptance can manifest itself as cockiness, a common trait of Jesuit high school students that is often misunderstood. Gillick says that ini-tially, Jesuit high school students typically are "above the median in being afraid." They've heard how tough the schools are, and they fear failure. Parents are pressuring them to do well in order to get into a good college. Societal messages reinforce their anxiety.

"Our culture asks kids to be afraid of not being liked and accepted," Gillick says. At this point, Jesuit schools intervene with messages that God and other people love these students so that they begin to love themselves (as the Bible commands). When students absorb these messages and succeed in their demanding environment, they may seem cocky.

"We push the kids to be so confident that they look cocky, but they are really bold, confident, and self-assured," Gillick says. "The word *cocky* is a bad word for bold, confident, self-accepting, grate-ful, and aware." These students are reflecting the caring outlook of their schools. "They believe in redemption—that [God says,] I have not given up on creation and will redeem you from self destruction," Gillick says.

Self-acceptance allows students to "come to life" and move into the final stage of spiritual development—**donation**. "Jesuits have created high schools where people come to share their gifts as faculty and staff," says Gillick. "They are committed to transmitting a faith doing justice, not just teaching knowledge about the faith. Our emphasis is on how to live the faith. We have to bring these kids into the light." Students embrace this "faith doing justice" by fulfilling service requirements, taking immersion trips to poor countries and poor areas of the United States, and raising money for mission-related projects. Countless Jesuit high school alums who have absorbed this ethic continue to serve others throughout their lives, as the stories in this book illustrate.

Formal Religious Programs

Formal religious activities vary from school to school, but all Jesuit high schools require theology/religious studies/religious formation classes, operate campus ministry programs, and sponsor service programs. Campus ministry offices organize liturgies, prayer and faith-sharing activities, student and faculty retreats, and service programs.

Fr. James Stoeger, SJ, former principal of Brebeuf Jesuit Preparatory School, says that most Jesuit high schools are 80 to 90 percent Catholic, and "that is a very good thing," because "you want to have a school that is clearly Catholic but open to other faith traditions." Having students of other faith traditions in a majority Catholic school can enrich the community by exposing the Catholic students to other heritages that they will interact with in today's multicultural world. Schools with majority Catholic student populations are not under parental or financial pressure to downplay their Catholic identity, theology, and values, but when a school, like Brebeuf, is only half Catholic, the religious environment changes. Brebeuf promotes itself as "Jesuit, Catholic, and interfaith." (See the profile on page 147.) Non-Catholic parents and even board members sometimes become concerned at attempts to make the school more Catholic.

Stoeger, also a former provincial assistant for secondary education for the Chicago Province, says that typical liturgical offerings at Jesuit high schools include the following:

- Daily Masses, which "a few students and teachers attend"
- Weekly class Masses for each grade
- All-school Masses three or four times a year, such as the Mass of the Holy Spirit at the beginning of the year
- Mission Masses
- Baccalaureate Masses and/or pregraduation Masses for the entire school
- Team Masses before football games and other major athletic events

In addition, schools usually offer penance services during Lent and Advent and Masses or prayer services for special occasions or special-interest groups.

"If there is a serious tragedy going on in which a kid dies, the spiritual aspect is very powerful," says Stoeger. "These are powerful religious moments for the community."

Joining the Jesuits

God calls men to become Jesuits. But often this happens with the assistance of Jesuit high school faculty members, as the following alumni vocation journeys demonstrate.

Ben Krause, class of '99 at Creighton Prep, spent a year teaching at his alma mater as a "donné" to look more closely at Jesuit life before entering the Society. "For me, the vocation discernment process involved constant little steps of taking a look at this life and finding out, without making a full commitment, if it was right for me," Krause said in an article in *Creighton Prep Alumni News*. "Being a 'donné' was part of that. It was also an opportunity for me to give back to Prep. It was clear to me that whatever I was going to do in life, regardless of whether I joined the Jesuits, was not going to pay me the big bucks, so I at least wanted to give of my time to Prep before deciding on a definite path."

Prep played a key role in the decision of another alum to join the Society. Pat Douglas, class of '94, says he was first attracted to the Jesuit brotherhood because he noticed how Br. Mike Wilmot, SJ, and Br. Jerry Peltz, SJ, interacted with students. "They weren't hitting me over the head with Jesus, but they had a certain peace about them that I was intrigued by. They weren't preaching their faith but drawing people in by living their faith."

Retreats

Student and faculty retreats are an integral part of the spiritual life of all Jesuit high schools. St. Ignatius, the patron saint of retreats, developed the Spiritual Exercises to help people find and embrace God's will for them by withdrawing from their regular work and taking time for prayer and reflection. According to Stoeger, schools typically offer one-day faculty and staff retreats, mandatory retreats for freshmen, voluntary or required retreats for upperclassmen, and opportunities for faculty and staff to make the Spiritual Exercises or an abridged version, such as the Nineteenth Annotation Retreat, also called the Retreat in Everyday Life.

Today's student retreats are lively affairs—worlds away from the lectures and silent prayer of retreats of yore. They often feature service projects, games, rock music, pizza, arts and crafts, and outdoor activities in addition to prayer, liturgy, reflection, and faith sharing. "For students to grow in faith, a positive experience of community is essential," says Stoeger. Good retreats give students a sense of meeting God, help them reflect on the presence of Jesus in their lives, and allow them to form new friendships. Kairos retreats, based on Cursillos, are popular.

The freshman retreat is a watershed event in a student's life. For many students, it is a life-changing experience. About a dozen Jesuit high schools, including Strake Jesuit Preparatory School, use a freshman retreat that Creighton Prep created in the 1970s. The Prep Retreat (as everyone calls it) is an intense, overnight small-group experience run by upperclassmen that emphasizes witness talks, liturgy, reflection, prayer, singing, art, and recreational activities. At Creighton Prep, Fr. Jim Michalski, SJ, developed the concept of a student-led retreat and then found students to assume responsibility for it. "When I came to Prep, it was one of the few Jesuit schools that had not dropped required retreats. Most have reinstated them," says Fr. Michalski. He says that the retreat succeeds because it "empowers the upperclassmen," who spend months planning everything and then run all the activities. "The group leaders start to understand their faith from sharing it."

On the Friday before Strake Jesuit's freshman retreat, rock music resounded in the hallway outside the campus ministry office, but the musicians, Andrew Richard and Patrick Stoia, were in no danger of landing in Penance Hall; they were practicing hymns for the Mass. "We're doing 'Holy Is the Lord' and 'Hungry,' something the kids can identify with more than traditional hymns," said Andrew, who plays in a classic rock band. "This is a really good environment. We are a religious school, and you can be free about expressing your religion."

Retreat posters hung all over the school, and students in Fr. Mark Thibodeaux's freshman religion class prayed for its success. The final preretreat "pep rally" for leaders was held in a candlelit auditorium and featured silent prayer, student homilies, and contemporary music.

Because all freshmen must participate, schools are sensitive to the needs of non-Catholics. Strake Jesuit even sets aside a prayer room for Muslim students.

At Creighton Prep, more than one hundred older students assist with the annual retreat, beginning with being on the housekeeping "ground crew" as sophomores. On the first night of the retreat, freshmen have dinner at their group leader's home. Afterward, a priest comes to hear confessions. Parents and teachers write letters expressing their love for the students—something new for many fathers.

Michalski says that at first, "a lot of people thought we were crazy to have the kids in charge." Skeptics became believers when they saw the impact of the retreat on students.

Profile: Creighton Prep Alum Changes the Lives of Choir Members

Gene Klosner of Los Angeles has sung for Pope John Paul II at World Youth Day, entertained audiences at the Grand Ole Opry, conducted liturgical music workshops at parishes around the nation, and cowritten an acoustic pop rock Mass with his sister and musical partner, Cher Klosner.

But Klosner's most lasting impact may be on the low-income Mexican American teenage members of his choir at Our Lady of the Rosary Church in Paramount, California. He's helping some get into college instead of working at the local grocery store. He's taken others to New York to perform at an annual event commemorating the victims of 9/11. He takes all of them to a concert at Hollywood Bowl, fifteen miles and a world away from Paramount—the farthest some have been from home.

None of this was planned, says Klosner, class of '78 at Creighton Prep. It all stemmed from the most important lesson he learned as a leader of Prep's freshman retreat. "I found out you don't have to wait until someone says, You can do this. I found out I could lead. Prep gives you permission to lead, so you tend to step up." He returns to sing at the freshman retreat every year.

The Klosners started directing the Our Lady of the Rosary choir after conducting a liturgical music workshop there. "We took the choir, and it really expanded into a great group of kids. We've become like big brother and sister to kids who were missing fathers. It was a weird thing. The kids would go to church and the parents wouldn't."

When the Klosners found that choir membership motivates students to improve their grades, they organized trips to colleges and explained how to finance higher education. "We wanted to show them something [other than] the college down the street," says Klosner. "We showed them how to apply for grants and loans. A lot are scared of loans. We said that if you get into a good college, you'll get a job that will more than pay for the loan." Some choir alums have enrolled at Jesuit universities.

Klosner grew up singing in church, and his teachers at Prep included Fr. Bob Dufford, SJ, a member of the St. Louis Jesuits musical group and composer of the beloved hymn "Be Not Afraid." "I got this great training. Cher and I sang in the choir on [the St. Louis Jesuits album] *The Steadfast Love.*" At Prep, he got involved in music, retreats, Christian Life Community, and Teens Encounter Christ. In his senior year, Klosner started singing at the freshman retreat when weather forced the bonfire to be canceled. The sing-along became a permanent part of the retreat. "Every year, I see guys who are seventeen or eighteen and know what they are doing. They are guiding kids through a weekend and learning leadership. They are learning how to stand up for their rights and a brother's rights. They have convictions that I don't see in other kids. This is one way to teach random kids how to be men for others. You can feel the Holy Spirit."

Adult Spirituality

Jesuit provinces and high schools have expanded their efforts to educate lay faculty and staff members in Ignatian spirituality. All the schools have a deliberate orientation program for faculty and staff. Many schools have an Ignatian identity committee that reports to the board and helps it look seriously at its responsibility to keep the school Ignatian.

Schools hire teachers who support the Ignatian mission, including many alums of Jesuit high schools, who already understand the philosophy and the demands. Schools seek faculty who are willing to "educate the whole person" through coaching or supervising activities; contracts often require participating in retreats and other spiritual activities.

The Jesuit provinces hold events that integrate school staff into the work of the entire Society. In the Chicago Province, teachers come together for a two-to-three-day immersion program on Ignatius. The Chicago and Detroit provinces both subsidize pilgrimages to Ignatian sites in Spain and Italy. The Missouri and Wisconsin provinces cosponsor a retreat for new faculty at a retreat center near St. Louis.

Dave Archibald, class of '99, who teaches theology and Spanish at Marquette University High School, attended the retreat and says it was good to be able to discuss "the important issues" with theology teachers from other schools. "Students are receiving other messages from society. What are we trying to reach them with?"

Schools usually require faculty and staff to participate in Ignatian formation programs. At Fordham Prep, pretenure faculty must attend weekly sessions on Ignatian spirituality and pedagogy for five years, says Pat Deane, assistant dean of students and assistant football coach. After that, Fordham Prep sponsors an annual Ignatian retreat and offers other opportunities for Ignatian formation, such as making the Spiritual Exercises. As a result, the school has reinforced its Ignatian heritage, from which it had drifted during the 1990s. "A bunch of us wanted to get back in touch with our Ignatian heritage," says principal Bob Gomprecht. The first step was a "workshop" featuring noted church historian John O'Malley, SJ. It was so successful that the next year, the school called the "workshop" a retreat. Now the annual Ignatian retreat is a highlight of the year.

At St. Ignatius Prep in San Francisco, an office of adult spirituality educates faculty and board members about Ignatian spirituality and sponsors prayer groups, a Lenten series, an Advent series, and lunches for discussing the Ignatian approach to life. Mary Abinante, of the campus ministry staff, says that the adult spirituality office helps "the adults in the community understand Ignatian spirituality. The Jesuit community diverted its financial support into this office. Otherwise, how will this school be Jesuit if there are no Jesuits? We've had a few [faculty members] do the thirty-day retreat, and more do an eight-day Ignatian retreat. More than a few have done the nineteenth annotation retreat."

Profile: Campus Minister Shows Priesthood Is Exciting

Before Thaddaeus Lancton met Fr. Mark Thibodeaux, SJ, at Strake Jesuit High School, he had never known a young priest who was full of energy and "excitement about being a priest."

"[Thibodeaux's] ability to be at the students' level, to be able to interact with them in a normal setting, is what impacted me most," says Lancton, who entered the Jesuits but left. "He knows how to be serious about serious things as a priest saying Mass, but he could make us laugh and have a good, clean time."

One year, four of the New Orleans Province's eleven novices were connected with Thibodeaux and/or Strake Jesuit. Thibodeaux's vocation groups introduce students to Jesuit life. Fr. Marvin Kitten, SJ, vocation director for the New Orleans Province, calls Thibodeaux "a good case for cloning."

Thibodeaux grew up in a Cajun Catholic Louisiana town wanting to be a priest, although he "hardly knew what a Jesuit was" until a teacher at his public high school suggested he become one. He had never visited the New Orleans Province novitiate, located only eleven miles from his home. When he called the novitiate, he asked, "What's a Jesuit? I think I want to be one." He has never looked back, even when he was a terrified Scholastic facing his first classes at the Jesuit College Preparatory School of Dallas.

"I would wake up in the middle of the night screaming 'I hate them [the students],'" he said. Thibodeaux asked for an assignment change but returned to Dallas Jesuit after praying in the novitiate's graveyard during a summer retreat. He could almost hear the early Jesuits who had fought Louisiana's swamps and alligators telling him "You're fine." He ended up loving Dallas Jesuit so much that he delayed his ordination a year to remain there. During his years at the school, he began writing about prayer, because he couldn't find suitable materials for one of his courses. Since then, he has written two popular books, *Armchair Mystic* and *God, I Have Issues*.

Thibodeaux joined Strake Jesuit in 2001, and 2005–06 was his last year there; the following year, he left for Tertianship, the final phase of Jesuit formation. A student in his freshman theology class prayed that "Fr. Thibs" would remember his students after leaving the school.

That prayer will be answered. Thibodeaux keeps in touch with alums. "When I fly into a given city, I get a list of what kids go to what colleges, and I go out with them at all hours of the night. One time [in Chicago], my cell phone rang at 12:30 a.m. Two or three of my students and I walked half an hour to an all-night diner and had pancakes at 3:30 a.m. We saw a kid wearing a Kairos cross. He was from Detroit Jesuit."

Strake Jesuit students weren't the only ones mourning Thibodeaux's anticipated departure from the school. He was too. "I love it. I would spend every day of my life in a high school."

Boards and Ignatian Mission

More boards are educating themselves about Ignatian mission and identity. St. Xavier High School in Cincinnati is a model of this approach.

The St. Xavier board starts every meeting with a presentation that showcases the school's Ignatian mission. A student might talk about a Kairos mission trip, or a retreat team captain might talk about the leadership skills required to run a retreat. Steve Hils, class of '71, who began the presentations when he was board president, says that they "set a tone for our meetings so we don't get buried in business. We talk about *magis*, but we need to think about *magis* for our board. We can't expect seventeen-year-olds to get it if we don't. The board's role will be to become more committed to priorities that enrich St. Xavier traditions. It is the board members' responsibility to balance the financial demands of the school with the needs they serve."

There also are practical benefits to this approach. Board members who understand the mission are more effective fund-raisers, because they can better explain the school's needs. "When we touch the heart, [the board members] want to know what they can do to make the school better," Hils says. Mission-driven gifts are larger and take more time to cultivate, because they involve moving "people into a deeper relationship with the school."

Hils, an insurance broker, says he believes that schools like St. Xavier have a "triple bottom line" that includes the way they treat students, parents, alumni, employees, and others and their impact on society.

Board leaders need to attend JSEA and provincial Ignatian leadership training events. "For boards not to be involved would be a failure," Hils says.

Profile: Brebeuf: Jesuit, Catholic, and Interfaith

Brebeuf Jesuit Preparatory School, in Indianapolis, promotes itself as Jesuit, Catholic, and interfaith—a coed school that welcomes students of all backgrounds and invites them to deepen their own faiths, says Sarah Steele, class of '93, the school's admissions director. "If you are Catholic, that's part of Brebeuf, but if you are Jewish or Protestant, this is also a school for you. You can celebrate that without feeling like an outsider."

Only half of Brebeuf's students are Catholic, which explains much of its variance from other Jesuit schools. Indianapolis has no Jesuit college or parish and is only about 10 percent Catholic. Students come from more than fifty feeder schools, half of them Catholic. Several non-Catholic private middle schools and junior high schools allow Brebeuf to recruit in their buildings and encourage their students to enroll in Brebeuf because of its academic excellence and interfaith reputation. Some people fear that if Brebeuf becomes more Catholic, the school's enrollment and fund-raising campaigns might be threatened. Others, including the Indianapolis Archdiocese and some parents, are pressing Brebeuf to strengthen its Catholic identity.

The differences between Brebeuf and other Jesuit schools are striking. Brebeuf opens the school year with an interfaith prayer service instead of a Mass. It requires students to take courses in world religions, morality, and social justice but not Scripture or dogma. Retreats are optional, and there is no Mass at the Kairos retreat. Common areas display minimal religious art.

But like other Jesuit schools, Brebeuf stresses service, and nearly all the students I interviewed had exceeded their service requirements. The school offers immersion trips to El Salvador and Ecuador. Each school day opens with a prayer over the PA system and closes with an *examen* (a traditional Jesuit examination of conscience). One day ended with a Catholic funeral prayer for the principal's father in addition to the *examen*.

A group of seniors (class of '06) gathered by campus ministry praised the impact of Brebeuf's interfaith culture on their lives. "The Jesuit ideals are universal," said Vinaya Vasudeva, a Hindu. "They can be applied to every religion. Brebeuf challenges you to question things you have heard or already know."

Emily Smith, an Episcopalian, said that she feared that "coming here, they would push the Catholic faith on me." Instead, "they push the Jesuit faith on you. The Jesuit ideals flow to every religion." Natalie McCain, a Catholic, credited Brebeuf with making her think about social justice issues, such as capital punishment, that her public grade school had never mentioned. "Here people were talking about it in the hallways. I never even knew I had a voice." Several students said that Brebeuf had strengthened their religious identities. For example, a Jewish student now went regularly to synagogue, which she had never done before.

Some school officials are trying to strengthen Brebeuf's Catholic identity, insisting that "Jesuit" must include "Catholic." Fr. Thomas Widner, SJ, the school's rector and head of a board Jesuit identity committee, says, "We must remain respectful [of all traditions] but strengthen and clarify our identity. We can't take our Jesuit/Catholic identity for granted. We have a very vague sense of identity. We are trying to get a discussion going of the interfaith thing. Some people are concerned that we are getting too Catholic again. Some want it to be more of an independent private school."

Widner says Brebeuf is enhancing the theological content of religion courses and activities. More than twenty faculty members signed up for an eight-week version of the Spiritual Exercises, and the school has begun hiring for mission.

5

Discipline

....

The teacher who influenced me more than any other at
Canisius High School was a short, tough, cigar-smoking, dark-
haired priest with a receding hairline who bore the menacing
title of Prefect of Discipline. Father John Sturm was a stocky
man with huge, Popeye-like forearms; people said he had once
been a Golden Gloves boxer, although nobody knew for sure.
He roamed the halls like a drill sergeant, which was fitting
because Canisius was to other high schools more or less what
the Marines are to other branches of the service: difficult,
demanding, and proud.

Father Sturm was always searching for signs of trouble,
and if trouble was lurking anywhere in the vicinity, he usually
found it. More often, though, he discouraged bad behavior
before it began. . . . All day long he barked out orders: "Stand
up straight." "Fix your tie." "Close your mouth." "Stay in line."
"Stand outside my office." And questions. . . . His persistent,
powerful, prosecutorial style elicited fast and honest responses
even from those who hadn't planned to tell the truth. It didn't
really matter whether he actually had evidence of our guilt.
What mattered was that we thought he did.

Tim Russert, class of '68,
Canisius High School, *Big Russ & Me*

Three months into their freshman year, Strake Jesuit's newest students were already awed by Br. Casey Ferlita, SJ, the school's disciplinarian.

"Br. Casey is very scary. He can be in eight places at once. He knows what you are going to do before you do it. He has the punishment planned," said Bradley Cayc. "Once, I cut across the grass, and he made me kiss it," said Kyle Pepper.

"He will make you own up to stuff you haven't done," said Cayc.

But students also already sensed Br. Casey's love for them. "We had a huge conversation about my aunt and her sons who came here," said Martin Smith. "Br. Casey is a brother, but he's also a father. He knows the right thing for everyone," said E. J. Neese.

Don't worry, alumni: the paddles and corporal punishment may be gone, but discipline—firm, tough, and ultimately loving—remains the trademark of Jesuit high schools, along with academic excellence. JUG (which some say stands for "justice under God"), PH (Penance Hall, in the New Orleans Province), and Saturday school are alive and well.

At Jesuit high schools, disciplinarians provide a "culture of support" that students may gripe about but are grateful for later. They are fortunate. Troubled adolescents today too seldom receive the care and guidance they need.

The mission of disciplinarians at Jesuit high schools is to get troubled students "back on track." These disciplinarians—especially older Jesuits, such as Br. Douglas Draper, SJ, of St. Ignatius Prep in San Francisco and Br. Casey Ferlita—are among their school's most memorable figures.

Profile: Br. Casey Ferlita, SJ

Br. Casey Ferlita, SJ, held up a computer printout containing the names of Strake Jesuit College Preparatory School students getting Ds or Fs in any of their classes. "This is my bible that I carry." Br. Casey keeps an eye out for these students when he patrols the hallways during class changes, because they are most likely to be in trouble.

"You have to be a presence. You have to make yourself seen. You have to get to know kids by their first names. You have to know the schedules of the kids. You have to know which kids are supposed to be in study hall. You can spot people who are not supposed to be where they are. I have to size up who is messing around. I have to hit the parking lots."

Br. Casey, who has been Strake Jesuit's disciplinarian since the mid-1970s, says that Ignatian-style discipline begins with love.

"Discipline starts with concern for the students," he says. "I look at the students as my brothers." However, his love can be tough. "He's a former boxer, and everyone knows it," says one alum.

Br. Casey says he sometimes tells a student, "Hey, boy, you are acting stupid" and sometimes uses four-letter words if he knows the student well and thinks the shock of it will teach accountability, responsibility, and communication.

"The kids who get in trouble are not communicating. I tell them that one of these days, you will work for someone and have to be accountable. That means being on time, following a dress code, and respecting people's property."

Br. Casey says that his brand of tough love is modeled on St. Ignatius's approach. "Ignatius was real regimental. We are all created to praise and serve God. The kids are trying to find themselves. They are all confused by all the peer pressure in their lives.

"The kids have to find themselves. That's the heart of Ignatian spirituality. Discipline *is cura personalis*. I see these kids, the ones who have so much trouble finding their niche. When they do, that's my gratification. They need to be guided. We have to work with them."

Students revere Br. Casey because "there's a world of difference between tough love and meanness," says Mike Doyle, class of '83, a past president of the alumni organization. "The guys having the most problems are the ones he's had the most impact on," Doyle says. PH and Saturday PH (equivalent to Saturday school) can help make boys feel "loved and cared about" when they need it most. For example, Br. Casey gave one boy whose parents were getting divorced several Saturday PHs more than his offenses deserved just to spend additional time with him.

Strake Jesuit alums have named their annual day of service after Br. Casey. "He's someone we can all relate to. [When we were] freshmen, he kept us in line and taught us the rules and regulations of Jesuit. At one time or another, he caught all of us in the parking lot when we weren't supposed to be there," says Todd Lorenz, class of '88 and a current member of the alumni board. Service-day projects typically involve heavy-duty maintenance work at inner-city Catholic grade schools and attract a cross section of alums.

St. Ignatius on Discipline

In *The Spiritual Exercises*, St. Ignatius paints powerful images of fire and brimstone. From his scandalous early life, he understood temptation. However, he also learned that temptation could be overcome. He was optimistic about the potential to conquer sin, but he was always aware of the consequences of failure.

In his book *Stretched for Greater Glory*, Fr. George Aschenbrenner, SJ, says that St. Ignatius urged kindness to those experiencing temptations and offered an "empowering message that trainees will not be left cowering, miserable and helpless against the satanic onslaught." Ignatian discipline is designed to help students become self-aware and take stock of their personal weaknesses in order "to overcome oneself and to order one's life," says Chris Lowney in *Heroic Leadership*.

Jesuit discipline has a long tradition. The *Ratio Studiorum* forbade "coming to school with swords or knives" and ordered students not to deface furniture. Students had to attend class faithfully and follow teachers' study plans diligently. There is consistency among Jesuit schools with respect to rules, expectations, and consequences because the schools have a common spirituality. Today's disciplinarians cite key phrases from *The Spiritual Exercises* when they describe their mission:

- To order one's life
- Discernment
- Becoming accountable
- *Magis*
- *Cura personalis*

Profile: Br. Douglas Draper, SJ

In 1973, an unsanctioned post-prom party was in full swing at an off-limits San Francisco hotel when students from St. Ignatius Prep heard a knock on the door: room service. A bright-eyed, smiling bellhop in a green uniform pushed a champagne cart into the suite.

Panic! "Br. Draper!" gasped a student. Attendees frantically pushed their dates into the bathroom and tried to hide under the beds. They were unwilling participants in the most famous episode of the legendary disciplinarian's career.

"I had heard that a group of students had rented the penthouse of a downtown hotel," says Draper. "I went to the manager, and he wouldn't cooperate. We have a lot of alums who are cops, so I called some of them on the bunco squad. The manager called back and said, 'What do you need?'" The green coat, the drink cart, and the suite number, thank you—ingredients for a prom night that will live in infamy.

Draper, the dean of American Jesuit school disciplinarians, has been administering "justice under God" at St. Ignatius Prep since 1969. Although corporal punishment was the norm at Jesuit high schools at that time, he never practiced it, because he thought it was "degrading." The office plaque with mounted handcuffs and a billy club is strictly symbolic. He prefers to outwit students.

Take, for example, the year that some St. Ignatius students celebrated homecoming by scattering trash on the lawn of a rival Catholic school. That school's disciplinarian called Draper and offered a clue about the perpetrators. "I'm afraid there isn't much to go on, but one of our teachers heard the boys call out to one friend, 'Joe, hurry up.'"

With just this clue, Draper described the incident over the PA system and reminded students how badly the episode violated St. Ignatius's standards. "So I want Joe and his friends to come to my office immediately," he concluded. And they did.

Draper became disciplinarian at St. Ignatius almost accidentally. He had completed formation just as the Jesuits opened educational careers to brothers, and he expected to be assigned to a school, possibly as a librarian. But despite his degree from the University of California at Berkeley, he was not among the "guinea pigs."

Soon after this, Draper complained about being overlooked for the school assignment while eating at a restaurant whose curtained booths concealed diners. Unbeknownst to him, his provincial was sitting at the next table and heard every word. The next day, the provincial appointed Draper assistant disciplinarian of St. Ignatius and then promoted him to disciplinarian the following year.

On Draper's first day as disciplinarian, he noticed some students fooling around, stepped outside, blew his whistle, and felt something hit his back. He was sure he had been shot.

Wrong.

"The principal told me, 'Someone threw an orange at you, and it's all over your cassock,'" Draper says. "I was never again afraid of kids."

Over the years, he has dealt with many incidents, such as the 1974 hilltop keg party in Golden Gate Park that he and a fellow Jesuit broke up. After pouring out the keg, Draper found he could not walk down the hill because of his cassock. A student hoisted the disciplinarian on his back and carried him down.

Draper used to ride with the San Francisco police on weekends, identifying the St. Ignatius students and taking over from there. "Perhaps the police were overburdened. My belief is that they knew that Brother would discipline [the students] in a fair way that might be more than they would face from the police," says Fr. Thomas Merkel, SJ, president of Creighton Prep and a former assistant disciplinarian at St. Ignatius.

Draper became a fixture at St. Ignatius's weekly bingo games, which attracted the school's elderly neighbors, many of them Jewish. After the 1989 earthquake, fire and police officials set up an emergency center at St. Ignatius and asked Draper to go door-to-door with them to evacuate the elderly. Police reassured residents that the "bingo priest" was there to take them to St. Ignatius Prep.

As the evacuees waited nervously at a staging area for their bus, an officer tried to calm them. "Ladies and gentlemen," he announced over the PA system, "as we wait for the bus, the bingo priest will lead you in the rosary." Many of the elderly Jewish women joined Br. Draper in praying "Holy Mary, mother of God . . ."

In 2000, Pope John Paul II presented Draper with the Pro Ecclesia et Pontifice medal for distinguished service to the church and the pope.

"I was certainly humbled by this honor, but I wasn't really struck by the significance of it until SI's Mass of the Holy Spirit when the student body gave me a standing ovation," says Draper. "I chose to live this commitment to Christ in a praying community of men who are engaged in ministry with service to their fellow brothers and sisters. I felt called to share my talents and gifts with others in a temporal way."

Draper has done far more than this, says Merkel. "He taught me so much about having love for the students. It was clear to me that the love was mutual. Freshman students feared [him], and senior students adored him. The students often had assemblies and they often imitated Brother, his walk and his gestures. Imitation is the greatest form of praise."

Hallmarks of Jesuit School Discipline

Rules governing such things as dress codes and punctuality are designed to develop the disciplined behavior that pays off in adulthood. Typical Jesuit high school rules include:

- If you come late to school or to class, chew gum, or violate the dress code, plan on JUG or PH. So there was heavy traffic? Anticipate problems and leave home earlier. Someday you'll have to be on time for work and dressed appropriately even if it is snowing or there's a traffic jam.
- If you misbehave in class or get in a fight, expect to go to JUG or PH or Saturday school. At Saturday school, you'll probably clean the school or do yard work. You also will spend one-on-one time with your disciplinarian.

- If you violate a major rule—for example, if you use alcohol or drugs—expect suspension from school and/or extracurricular activities.

Jesuit schools are direct about rules and consequences. David Laughlin, president of St. Louis University High School and former disciplinarian at Creighton Prep, sums up the common view: "We believe in honest communication. We say to students, 'This is expected.' Discipline is the foundation for maximizing our God-given talents. Accountability involves not only what we don't do but the *magis*—the more. We are obligated to be of service. What's distinctive is that it is founded on the idea of *cura personalis*. These are not just policies. We are helping students develop themselves. We have an image of tough love. We understand that what is in someone's best interest is not always the most pleasant."

Laughlin says that Ignatian disciplinarians weigh two factors in handling problems: rules and policies stated in handbooks, and the students' needs. Cases cannot be handled in exactly the same way, because no two students' needs are the same.

"It's not a perfect science," Laughlin says. There is often room for flexibility. Disciplinarians try to help students learn from their mistakes and problems. Parents are usually grateful for this approach. For example, a mother whose son was treated for alcoholism still volunteers for his school, because it provided tutors who enabled him to graduate with his class. In return, the boy helped counsel other alcoholic students and their parents.

Laughlin says that students are expelled from Jesuit high schools when their absence from school is necessary for their growth and when their conduct jeopardizes the safety of the school community or other students.

Administrators often debate the greater good when deciding how to handle issues. Says Laughlin: "Our schools are known for making tough decisions. We have to care enough to act. Ignatius believed in the multiplier effect. We are preparing students to be leaders of the community. Discipline is a core part of this."

Most schools take a similar approach to discipline, although a few vary from the norm. For example, most Jesuit schools have fairly strict dress codes. Some require ties for males, and most ban jeans. Cristo Rey schools require professional dress.

At Red Cloud High School, conventional JUG wouldn't work, because the buses that students take home run on tight schedules to all corners of a reservation the size of Rhode Island.

Profile: "Top" and the Uniform

Not all legendary disciplinarians are Jesuits. Lawrence Abshire, prefect of discipline at New Orleans Jesuit High School, is known simply as Top, a legacy of his previous career as a marine master sergeant. New Orleans Jesuit requires students to wear a uniform rather than follow a dress code, as many other Jesuit schools do. Abshire governs his khaki-clad charges with military precision.

"His favorite phrase is 'Gentlemen, we're going to do this in an orderly fashion,'" says Ian Gunn, class of '07.

Students assigned to PH meet after school to copy pages from their handbook. "Top is walking around, saying 'Write faster.'" Violators of the uniform rules (khaki dress shirts and pants with a brass belt buckle, black dress shoes, black socks, and name tags) receive PH. Gunn has been cited for such things as scratches on his belt buckle. During the semester when he was displaced by Hurricane Katrina, Gunn lived under

Strake Jesuit's more relaxed dress code and found, to his surprise, that he missed the uniform.

"Kids asked if [we] could wear our Jesuit uniforms. It's part of home and who we are," he says. "In New Orleans, when you see someone in that uniform and walk into a job interview wearing it, you're hired instantly. People are looking forward to wearing their uniforms. It brings us closer. Alums see our uniforms and ask about teachers."

JUG at Red Cloud

JUG is one of the first terms most freshmen at Jesuit high schools learn, but the disciplinarian at Red Cloud High School had never heard of it. "What's JUG?" asked Nick Dressel, assistant principal for students.

Red Cloud High School uses the "step system" of discipline, a legacy of its history as a boarding school. Students are typically detained after class for a minute or two for minor offenses, depriving them of socializing time between classes. More serious offenses result in stiffer penalties, including in-school suspension and expulsion.

6

Student Life

In chess you compete completely based on your rating. Two of our kids lost to two younger girls. They were devastated. It dealt a blow to their egos due to the gender difference. It was a great chance for a discussion of how they saw themselves as males versus girls. This experience and the ability to reflect on it was a great preparation for life.

John Raslowsky,
assistant for secondary education, New York Province,
and former principal, St. Peter's Prep

Jesuit schools offer a bewildering smorgasbord of sports and activities, because they teach life lessons under the guise of football, band, or photography. "Students enter by their door and leave by ours," says John Raslowsky, echoing an Ignatian proverb.

Whether the "door" is chess, basketball, theater, music, photography, or Science Olympics, faculty mentors use the activity to teach discipline, accountability, and leadership. "Cocurriculars are the glue for the larger school community, but they also are a community within a community. Students join with other kids with shared goals. Cocurricular activities are a way to be in a relationship with kids," Raslowsky says.

Supervising teams and activities allows teachers "to show care and concern for every student. They extend our reach beyond class to areas of interest to students," says Fr. Don Petkash, SJ, Detroit Province assistant for secondary education.

Typical Cocurricular Programs

Jesuit Scholastics and lay teachers often put in the equivalent of a second shift coaching and supervising organizations. They're continuing an Ignatian tradition that dates to the sixteenth century, when the Jesuits invented Europe's first cocurricular activities.

The size of Jesuit high schools facilitates this commitment. About 80 percent have eight hundred to twelve hundred students, small enough that few students go unnoticed but large enough to accommodate diverse interests. Typical Jesuit high schools have thirty to fifty clubs in addition to numerous sports, campus ministry programs, and class-related activities such as forensics, music, and student publications. At most Jesuit schools, teachers and counselors constantly encourage students to get involved. Raslowsky says that typical cocurricular offerings include:

- Campus ministry/retreat/pro-life clubs
- Service organizations
- Drama, speech, and debate
- Ethnic or cultural clubs
- A variety of music options, including choir and other choral groups, jazz band, orchestra, and occasionally marching band
- Student publications, including yearbook, newspaper, and literary magazine
- Academic clubs for various disciplines, competitive academic groups such as Academic Decathlon team or Science Olympic team, and foreign language groups

- Computer and other technology clubs
- Sports, sports, and more sports, both interscholastic and intramural

At Rockhurst High, for example, there's a club for everything, including sitting on benches during lunch (the Bench Club). Here is Rockhurst's catalog of clubs: Amnesty International, Bench Club, Best Program, Bicycle Club, Black Box Productions, Book-of-the-Month Club, Brothers Program, Chapel Choir, Chess Club, Choir Council, Classics Club, Computer Club, Debate, Drama Club, Eilert Ecology Club, Engineering Club, Fellowship of Christian Athletes, "FIAT" Club, Flying Club, French Club, Freshman Retreat, Herpetology Club, Hockey Club, Intramurals, Investment Club, Kairos Fourth Day, Latin Club, Math Club, Multiethnic Education Team, National Honor Society, Pastoral Council, Pep Band, *Prep News*, Pro-Life Club, The Quarry, Racquetball Club, Regis Club, *Rock Collection*, Science Club, Spanish Club, Spirit Club, Student Government Association, Students against Drunk Driving, Students for Political Action, TIE—Total Ignatian Experience, Ultimate Frisbee Club, Video Club, Visual Arts Club, Volleyball Club, Work Grant, and Yell Leaders.

In addition to these are a number of sports: baseball, basketball, cross-country, football, golf, hockey, lacrosse, soccer, swimming, tennis, track and field, and wrestling.

The efforts to get students involved pay off. During their exit interviews, seniors repeatedly describe the school as a "brotherhood" and a "fraternity." "They all defend RHS to a fault. There is a very obvious pride in RHS and strong relationships with peers and faculty," says assistant principal for student affairs Michael Heringer.

Grateful parents cite the role of cocurricular activities in helping their children identify future careers. For example, Brian Gray, editor of the National Catholic Educational Association's *Momentum* magazine, noted that his son, Brendan, joined the stage crew at Gonzaga College

High School because his carpool driver was on stage crew. By senior year, Brendan was stage manager and received a service award. This led to his career in theater lighting and commercial events. Today he runs a lighting design firm in Manhattan.

Profile: Chris Bosco

Chris Bosco is a pastoral associate and an English teacher whom students revere despite his difficult courses. Bosco, a graduate of St. Louis University High School, class of '95, helps coach track and field, directs the freshman retreat, moderates a National Honor Society tutoring program, and is co-moderator of the Yell Leaders. During track season, he spends three hours a day coaching and attends meets on weekends.

"Real school begins after the 3:00 p.m. bell," he says. "We are here for the whole person. It is stated very clearly that you will be here for the whole person. Extracurriculars give students a more realistic sense of what it means to be a complete person." Supervising extracurricular activities "gives the teacher the chance to reflect the same ideals beyond the classroom. I don't think a Jesuit school would work if it weren't set up like this," he says, adding that freshmen relate differently to him in the spring, when he becomes "Coach Bosco," than in the fall, when he's just "Mr. Bosco."

He continues coaching because "there's something new every day," and he gets rewards from working with athletes and fellow coaches that his wife doesn't get in her business job.

Profile: Mike Wickenhauser

Mike Wickenhauser is also an English teacher, whose cocurricular assignments include supervising the literary magazine and helping coach varsity soccer. A graduate of De Smet High School, class of '91, he also directs Kairos retreats, chairs the faculty development committee, and works with the Student Success Center and Rockhurst's North Central accreditation steering committee.

"If all I did was teach, I would just have an academic relationship with students," he says. "To forge a relationship, you need to consider the student as a person."

Wickenhauser says that by coaching soccer and directing the Kairos retreat, he forms ties with students that allow him to help them with concerns about their parents, girlfriends, and college decisions. The hours are rough. Soccer season means three hours of practice a day plus four hours on Saturday. The literary magazine also demands many hours beyond class. However, the rewards are worth the time.

"I speak with a lot of people in business," Wickenhauser says. "When I go to an office, I don't sense the excitement as to what will happen. My wife is in corporate PR, and she envies the fact that my work matters. I can say something to a kid, and he will be grateful for the advice. There's the opportunity every day to feel good about ourselves. I'm a better teacher because of my involvement in extracurriculars."

The Ignatian Value of Sports

Jesuit schools are usually athletic powerhouses that emphasize both success and widespread participation. Officials see athletic success as part of overall school excellence—the *magis*. It promotes pride, parent and alumni loyalty, and donations. At many schools, a majority of students play at least one sport.

Contrary to urban myth, Jesuit schools don't award athletic scholarships, and varsity athletes must meet standard academic requirements. However, Jesuit schools have built-in advantages when it comes to athletics, including traditions of success and the ability to draw students from a wide area. "The Jesuits like to succeed on all levels, including athletics and raising money," says Daniel P. Costello, class of '72, vice president for advancement at Gonzaga College High School. "Part of being a Jesuit school is to raise money and succeed athletically."

Football even helped save Gonzaga when riots in its neighborhood drastically cut enrollment in the early 1970s. The school built a football field to rally alumni support and to signal its determination to remain in its historic location near the U.S. Capitol. A few years later, Gonzaga built a new gym to replace an ancient basketball court whose boundaries were the wall of the school. Today's Gonzaga is stronger than ever. It can accept only about a third of its applicants.

Students make good use of the football field and the gym. About 70 percent of the students play a sport at one time or another. Gonzaga offers about twenty sports, including club sports such as squash and water polo. "Most of the time, guys do better academically during their seasons," says Michael Howell, class of '70, an academic dean who has coached baseball. "They don't have much time, so they have to focus and organize better. Our philosophy is that if you are able to stay in school, you can play a sport."

Football, basketball, baseball and softball, track, cross-country, and soccer are staples at most Jesuit schools. Hockey, wrestling, swimming, lacrosse, tennis, and golf are important in some regions. Often schools have multiple teams or no-cut teams in some sports to allow students to participate regardless of ability. Intramurals are popular in sports like basketball and soccer, which have small varsity squads.

"Athletics at their best are a way for kids to see God at play in the world," Raslowsky says.

Sports "Develop" Their Schools

A former longtime Gonzaga College High School football coach and current chief fund-raiser Daniel Costello recounts a typical scenario at an alumni reunion:

He chats with a former player who has become an affluent doctor, attorney, or businessman, reminding him of his playing days. Instantly, the alum is sixteen again, and Costello is his coach. They reminisce about the fun and the glory days, but then Costello might kid about the big game that the alum has never forgotten—the awful day that his offside penalty cost Gonzaga the game.

The alum will give Gonzaga whatever Costello asks for.

Jesuit schools reap long-term financial benefits from the hours that teachers spend coaching all those teams, says Costello. "The athletic part of high school is the message that sticks, especially in an all-boys school. Men hold on to it their whole lives. At reunions they mostly talk about their old teams, especially football. With the Jesuits, anything that is worth doing they do well." Success in athletics is "huge to development," Costello says, and "football drives the car."

Costello notes that no matter how powerful and successful his former players have become, he's still "Coach" to them. They still seek his approval. "When we have a campaign, I'll go ask these kids for money, and no one says no, because there's such a strong bond. A lot of our best contributors are former athletes."

Parents also bond with a school through athletics, he says. "If their sons are happy, they are more likely to be your contributors. [Former president] Fr. Bernard Dooley used to say that your endowment is walking in your halls. If you have genuine learning, excitement, and fun, you'll have [the students] for life. If you make the kids happy, their parents can't do enough for the school."

Alums often show their gratitude for long-ago kindnesses with generous gifts.

Gonzaga has received "hundreds of thousands" of dollars from an alum who couldn't afford a winter coat when he was a student, says president Fr. Allen Novotny, SJ. The alum, who made a fortune in business, has never forgotten the cold day when former longtime athletic director Joe Kozik gave him a heavy Gonzaga jacket. The alum tells Gonzaga that he's still paying for the coat.

Some superstar athletes also repay their schools. For example, Cy Young Award–winning pitcher David Cone, class of '81 at Rockhurst High, made one of the school's biggest gifts, directing that "a major portion be spent on improving athletic facilities," according to Roger Angell in *A Pitcher's Story: Innings with David Cone*. Rockhurst dropped baseball in 1966 to save money and had no baseball team when Cone was a student. At the time, he organized a petition drive to start one, but the school refused. Rockhurst restored baseball in 1989, after receiving Cone's gift.

Becoming Men and Women for Others

"Justice concerns" loom ever larger in Jesuit school cocurricular activities. Summer immersion service trips are common nationwide, as are service programs for the local poor.

"St. John's in Toledo has started a ministry to people in Guatemala who live in garbage dumps," says Fr. Don Petkash, SJ, assistant for secondary education in the Detroit Province and a former president of Walsh Jesuit High School, in Cuyahoga Falls, Ohio. "They have built a day-care center and are building a school where kids can be dropped off." Walsh Jesuit took students to Northern Ireland so they could "find out what it is like to be a minority. That opened kids' eyes to some of the greater problems."

St. Ignatius of Cleveland sponsors not only the pallbearer program described in this book's opening vignettes but also a Labre project, in which parents, students, and faculty distribute sandwiches to the homeless, get to know them by name, and form relationships with them. Gonzaga College High School has opened a Campus Kitchen to prepare and deliver meals to the elderly.

Numerous Jesuit high schools partner with local inner-city middle schools, and practically all Jesuit high schools sponsor groups to celebrate their students' ethnic heritages.

Seasonal food drives are widespread. In 2005, New Orleans Jesuit's Thanksgiving drive after Hurricane Katrina received national media coverage. Creighton Prep's annual Christmas Operation Others food drive, done in collaboration with other Omaha Catholic high schools, feeds fifteen hundred families a year.

Most justice-related programs emphasize reflection and discussion. For example, students participating in the annual Jesuit-sponsored protest at Fort Benning's School of the Americas—whose graduates assassinated six Jesuits in El Salvador—might discuss the costs of advocacy for the poor.

Mission Weeks at several Midwestern Jesuit schools raise funds for mission-related causes with games, student-faculty competitions, dances, and the like. De Smet High School in St. Louis has celebrated Mission Weeks for more than thirty years and raised about thirty thousand dollars in 2006. That same year, Creighton Prep raised twenty thousand dollars for Jesuit famine relief in Kenya, the local Jesuit middle school, and hurricane aid for Jesuit High School of New Orleans.

Ethnic Activities at Brebeuf

Brebeuf Jesuit Preparatory School, in Indianapolis, celebrates the diverse heritages of its students at festivals featuring their food and culture—an effort to "build a school community that feels welcoming and affirming," says director of diversity Freezell Brown. "Our festivals provide an annual occasion where kids feel they have a moment in the spotlight."

About 16 percent of Brebeuf's students are minorities. About a dozen of the school's fifty cocurricular organizations are diversity related. There are black, Asian, and Jewish cultural groups open to all students; Spanish, French, and German language/cultural clubs; and a Unity Club, focusing on gender orientation.

"These are places for kids to connect with the school community," says Brown. "There's a whole range of opportunities."

Brown, an African American from a lower-income family who holds two master's degrees, says cocurricular activities helped him feel valued in high school. "I went to one of the private schools in town. I played basketball all four years and managed the football team. I was heavily involved in vocal music, choir, and theater. I had multiple places where I connected to the school community, where I had a moment in the spotlight, and where I felt valued."

Brown says that the Lilly Endowment has funded Brebeuf's diversity training research and has underwritten a partnership with the Oaks Academy, a lower-income elementary school. Students, faculty, and staff volunteer for an after-school program that develops "organic relationships" between the two schools.

Social Life at an All-Male School

Question: Other than football, what do Rockhurst High students do for fun?

Answer: Sign up for activities with the girls from all-female St. Teresa's Academy and Notre Dame de Sion High School.

"We all come from coed grade schools," says Henry Thomas, class of '06. "I've heard all the bad stereotypes about all-guy schools, but I've come to love this. Guys are more open and honest with each other."

"I don't have to worry about how I act or personal hygiene," says Jeff Huggins, class of '07. "Things are easier to deal with."

"In our classrooms, we are a lot more focused," says Frank Reardon, class of '07. "Our teachers can be more open and honest without girls around," says Mark Fowler, class of '07.

Thomas says he gained added appreciation for single-sex education during a mission trip to Mexico, where he visited a coed high school and saw students "coming on" to each other during class. "I got a great grasp of how lucky we are. We're more focused and honest. We don't put on a show for the opposite sex."

Outside of class, Rockhurst students attend dances and football and basketball games with girls from St. Teresa's and Sion. The three schools also come together for music, theater, fund-raising activities, proms, church activities, and switch days, in which students visit each other's schools. Girls from St. Teresa's and Sion play the female roles in plays at Rockhurst, and vice versa. Many all-male Jesuit schools have such sister schools.

Rockhurst students say they enjoy a closer relationship with faculty than their friends at other schools, especially public schools, have with their faculty. The difference is visible at school functions. "Teachers at other schools stand to one side at school activities," says Thomas. "Ours are usually in the middle of students. You don't shy away from our teachers." The boys at Rockhurst say their friends who attend public schools are less involved in school activities and are less likely to wear school sweatshirts on weekends. Two boys mentioned that the vandalism or violence sometimes directed at teachers in public schools is unheard of at Rockhurst, because teachers help students solve personal problems and allow them to hang out in their offices.

All say their pride in Rockhurst stems from its outstanding reputation, its demanding academics, its athletic success, and their involvement in activities. "Kids look out for each other," says Thomas. "Everyone speaks to each other."

Profile: Jesuits Defeat Celtics

The Society of Jesus defeated the Boston Celtics in the competition for Earle Markey's services.

Fr. Markey, associate admissions director for the College of the Holy Cross, starred on the basketball team at St. Peter's Prep, in Jersey City, and accepted a basketball scholarship to Holy Cross after he graduated, in 1949. At the time, Holy Cross boasted one of the nation's top basketball programs. Markey, a five-foot-eleven guard, was a freshman at Holy Cross when one future Celtics Hall of Famer, Bob Cousy, was a senior, and Markey was a senior when another, Tommy Heinsohn, was a freshman.

Markey starred for Holy Cross for three years while majoring in English. The Celtics selected him in the fourth round of the 1953 NBA draft, but he joined the Jesuits instead.

Markey never looked back. His Jesuit assignments have included teaching in the Philippines, serving as principal of St. Peter's Prep, and serving as dean of students and vice president of student affairs at Holy Cross. He believes that high school sports can be a positive influence but cautions that they must be kept in balance with academics.

Basketball played an influential role in his life at St. Peter's Prep, he says. "It was a great joy and a release for me. There was the camaraderie of the team and the fun of getting to know people. It was quite demanding. You had a game on Saturday, and you still had to write an essay on Sunday. Sports are a microcosm of life. Your success depends on your dedication and talent."

But Markey warns that high school sports are experiencing a trickle-down effect from the professionalizing of college sports, which he decries. Many high school students are forced to specialize in one sport by junior high, because they join select teams that demand high fees, year-round training, and travel. In the 1940s, Markey says, almost anyone who tried out could make the St. Peter's Prep teams without special training. "High school sports are wonderful provided they are kept in balance and proportion and if you can keep up with the schoolwork."

Profile: Coach Exemplified Courage

Paul Straub, a former marine who lost both of his legs below the knee fighting on Guadalcanal, inspired half a century's worth of students at Tampa Jesuit, where he coached football, basketball, and track and served as athletic director and later as alumni director. Straub, who had been a football star at the University of Tampa before World War II, left rehabilitation determined to turn his loss into a gain for others. At Tampa Jesuit, which he joined in 1948, he did just that.

Lou Piniella, the Yankees baseball star who won a World Series as manager of the Cincinnati Reds and is currently manager of the Chicago Cubs, played baseball for Straub at Tampa Jesuit. "He showed me how to be a good athlete and a good person. He was always encouraging me. Of all the people who played a part in my success, he played the biggest," he said in a 1987 article in *Company* magazine.

In the same article, Adolph Hartschlag, of Jacksonville, spoke of how Straub had inspired him as well. Hartschlag, whose leg was blown off in Vietnam in 1965, said of Straub, "Here was a guy who loses both legs and comes back and helps out kids in high school, and you say, 'This guy's got something special.' I thought, If this guy can do it with two, why can't I do it with one?"

PART 2

SCHOOLS SERVING SPECIAL COMMUNITIES

7

The Cristo Rey Phenomenon

....

My dad went from garbage picking in Mexico to having a daughter going to Georgetown.

Karina Ramirez, class of '06,

Cristo Rey Jesuit High School, Chicago

In the Pilsen and Little Village community of Chicago's near Southwest Side, hardworking Mexican immigrants struggle to give their children a better life. They're blue-collar workers without a lot of extra cash. The two local public high schools are overcrowded and gang infested. The dropout rate for Hispanic teens in the area is more than 50 percent, and only about a third of those who graduate go on to college.

At low-income Cristo Rey Jesuit High School in the heart of Pilsen, however, all members of the class of 2006 were accepted into college, including Karina Ramirez, who was headed to Georgetown University to study nursing; Jimmy Mena, who planned to major in biology and chemistry at the University of Illinois; and Jacqueline Carillo, who planned to major in chemistry at the University of Chicago en route to a dental career.

Both Mena and Carillo won Gates Millennium scholarships that pay all undergraduate expenses for outstanding low-income minority students. They are part of one of the nation's most successful educational innovations, which started in 1996 with one word: *jobs*. Cristo Rey bills itself as "the school that works."

Like all of Cristo Rey's more than five hundred students, Ramirez, Mena, and Carillo paid most of their tuition through the Corporate Internship Program, in which they worked one day a week and one Monday a month for one of Cristo Rey's more than one hundred corporate sponsors. Sponsors contract with Cristo Rey to fill entry-level jobs. Four students (one from each grade level) rotate days and attend classes the remainder of the week. The sponsors pay Cristo Rey the salary the students have collectively earned. The school day is extended to make up for hours missed working. Through this winning plan:

- Cristo Rey obtains a reliable source of funding
- Students earn 70 percent of their tuition, allowing them to afford a Jesuit education (most also get financial aid for the remainder of the tuition, $2,650)
- Employers gain reliable workers for high-turnover jobs

This revolutionary solution to financing Catholic education in inner-city areas is spreading throughout the country through the Cristo Rey Network. At least a dozen cities have opened or plan to open similar Catholic high schools or have converted existing schools to the Cristo Rey model. These include Jesuit-run Arrupe High School, in Denver; Verbum Dei High School, in the Watts area of Los Angeles, which the Jesuits cosponsor with the Archdiocese of Los Angeles; and the new Jesuit Cristo Rey High School in Sacramento.

Birth of a Dream

The Cristo Rey movement began when Chicago's late cardinal Joseph Bernardin was seeking to better serve the city's massive and growing

Hispanic population. He asked the Jesuits to "bring educational excellence where it was needed most." For years, Catholic high schools nationally had been providing the best education available in inner-city neighborhoods, but in city after city, they were closing or relocating and not being replaced because of financial difficulties.

Despite the declining number of Jesuits available to launch new projects, the Chicago Province agreed to answer Bernardin's call. The Chicago provincial assigned Fr. Jim Gartland, SJ, who is fluent in Spanish, to do a feasibility study in the Pilsen and Little Village neighborhoods.

"I hit the streets," Gartland says. "I interviewed people at local churches and schools and sat down with business groups. I talked to kids on the streets and looked at census data. From listening, I found out that there were about ten thousand high school–age kids in the two neighborhoods and that the public school dropout rate was close to 75 percent. Only 3 percent of the adults had college degrees."

A new Jesuit high school could help, Gartland determined, but the families in the neighborhood could not afford the tuition the school would have to charge.

A Workable Solution

Finally, management consultant Richard Murray suggested finding jobs for students to finance their tuition. The next step was to persuade employers to hire inner-city teens for entry-level jobs in their offices—an idea so audacious that probably no one but the Jesuits would have tried it, let alone made it work.

For the jobs and donations needed to launch the new school, the Jesuits turned to their network of contacts: primarily alums of Jesuit universities and high schools, especially St. Ignatius College Prep (ten minutes and a world away) and Loyola Academy in suburban Wilmette, Illinois. Gartland (who is now the school's president) received assistance from his alma mater, St. Ignatius High School in Cleveland. The greater Jesuit alumni network responded, giving birth to Cristo Rey.

"We hear a lot of alums say they're from working-class families," says Gartland. "They identify with the history of Jesuit education for working-class families."

In a *60 Minutes* interview, Fr. John Foley, SJ, Cristo Rey's first president, said, "We went out and knocked on doors and said, Would you give us a job?—meaning would they give our students jobs." Today Cristo Rey can accept only a fourth of its applicants, but when it opened, "we grabbed kids off the street," Gartland says. The school provided employment orientation and transportation from school to jobs, many of them in Chicago's downtown area. The school dress code requires professional attire, including ties for boys, which is in keeping with the work-study program.

"When we sent them out to work the first day in 1996, I felt like hiding behind my desk," Foley said on *60 Minutes*. But the plan worked far better than anyone could ever have imagined.

Students at Work

Cristo Rey runs its own employment agency that finds jobs for all students at some of Chicago's most prestigious employers. Sponsors— including law, investment, and consulting firms; educational, cultural, religious, and health-care organizations; banks, insurance companies, and other corporations—commit to a certain number of jobs. The largest employer is Loyola University Health System, which in 2005–06 provided 10.5 jobs, shared by forty-two students.

The students' jobs include data entry, filing, and running errands, and they receive performance evaluations, just as adult employees do. One typical semester, more than 90 percent of the students earned "good" to "outstanding" performance ratings. They also gain maturity, self-confidence, professional role models and mentors, and exposure to the world outside Pilsen and Little Village.

Mena, Carillo, and Ramirez said they chose Cristo Rey because of its academics and the work-study program and because the total package offered them the best chance for the future. All three are the children of blue-collar Mexican immigrants. Their mothers stayed home to raise their families. They performed a variety of jobs during high school.

Mena worked at Jenner & Block, a law firm in downtown Chicago; Northwestern University; and the Loyola University Health System. Ramirez worked with the Catholic Church Extension Society. By her junior year, she was doing data entry for Cargill Investment Group, proud that "they would trust me with so much money." Carillo spent all four years working for a downtown law firm.

One student told the *Chicago Tribune* in 2003: "I'm sixteen years old and work in R. W. Baird's investment banking department. Do you know how that makes me feel? If I've done this by age sixteen, think what my future can be. Me, whose only job before this was helping my dad, a roofer, outside on the weekends."

Students sometimes work for their employers over Christmas breaks and during summer vacations and keep the salary they earn. Some continue to work for their employers during college, as alum Nicholas Morales did for McKinsey & Co. while he studied at Loyola University.

"When I started, I was intimidated," Morales told the *Tribune.* "Everyone was in business attire. I'd never seen anything like that before except on television. But they were friendly and encouraging. From not knowing anything about anything, now I'm on the computer desk answering questions from big shots in Germany and New York."

Praise for Cristo Rey

The Cristo Rey Network and its schools have received major grants and praise from some of the nation's largest foundations, notably the Bill and Melinda Gates Foundation, which in 2003 pledged close to ten million dollars to spread the concept to other cities. Many of the network schools are diocesan or run by other religious orders.

"Cristo Rey has created a powerful, innovative educational model," Marie Groark, senior policy officer at the Gates Foundation, told the *Chicago Tribune.* "It's bringing to America's poorest communities the three Rs: rigor, relationships, and relevance." The executive director of education at the Gates Foundation, Tom Vander Ark, said in *America* magazine that Cristo Rey is succeeding in a neighborhood where "there is a 65 percent public high school dropout rate. Ninety-two percent of the students in this area qualify for the federal free or reduced-price lunch program," and the "median family income of the students at Cristo Rey is $29,000 for a family of four."

Vander Ark said he had wondered if the work component would be a hardship for students, but "every interview indicated that the work experience was what the students liked best in the school's program. They appreciated their connection with the adult world and its work. They also valued the respect they received as a contributor to the work team."

Academically, he noted, Cristo Rey is a typical Catholic high school that "offers a college preparatory curriculum taught by dedicated teachers in a positive environment. Like all good high schools, it has a set of clear goals and high expectations concerning student performance."

Jay Mathews of the *Washington Post* suggested that the Cristo Rey model could resolve the national debate over funding private schools with vouchers. "Would the national debate over school vouchers sound different if the voucher money came not from taxpayers but from the useful money of students themselves?" he asked.

A Few Problems

For all its success, Cristo Rey Jesuit High School faces challenges, including retention, says Gartland. Currently, retention is at about 65 percent at Cristo Rey and 60 percent at other network schools. Gartland adds that "we want to see a retention of at least 80 percent." The school drops students who fail so many classes that they cannot make up the credits during summer.

Gartland says that about two-thirds of Cristo Rey's students come from public schools and initially struggle with study skills and organizational skills. There also are social problems, such as gangbangers, although most students are "great kids from great families." The school strictly enforces a rule against fraternizing with gang members. But Cristo Rey cannot escape the problems of its neighborhood. In 2004, a student was killed in a neighborhood shooting.

A counseling department wall display lists the problems students say they have faced, including bullies, gangs, rape, and verbal abuse. More than 60 percent get academic assistance because they have received at least two Ds, says Peter Beale-DelVecchio, development director.

Support from the Community

Cristo Rey's modern, attractive, spotless campus stands out in the middle of its aging neighborhood. A high-powered board of trustees and a prestigious leadership advisory council consisting of business leaders, attorneys, and others helped raise the twenty-six million dollars needed to construct the facility. The archdiocese contributed the school's site for a dollar. Cristo Rey has built several additions, and more work is planned. Some rooms remain unfinished until they are needed for the projected enrollment increase to six hundred, says Beale-DelVecchio.

"The support of the Jesuit schools is why this school got started," Gartland says. At a recent fund-raiser, 75 percent of those attending had Jesuit alumni connections.

Gartland notes that some were alums of Campion High School, a Jesuit boarding school in Wisconsin that closed years ago. Since they have no alma mater to support, some Campion alums, such as businessman Tom O'Brien, have adopted Cristo Rey as a substitute. O'Brien, whose auto company hires students, purchased a dinner for six with the Jesuits at the auction; he told Gartland that he planned to host Campion friends to get them involved with Cristo Rey.

Other Cristo Rey Schools

Arrupe Jesuit High School, Denver. Every day when students from Arrupe High School return from the jobs through which they are paying their tuition, Fr. Stephen W. Planning, SJ, the school's president, meets them and asks how their day went. If they say it was fine, he congratulates them, says Michael O'Hagan, the school's principal. If they say the day was horrible or boring, he tells them he's glad they don't like it. "He tells them to keep studying so [they] will have a career doing something meaningful," says O'Hagan.

Arrupe High School's mission is to open the doors to that meaningful future for low-income Denver students. The school is based on the Cristo Rey model and reverses a long, sad trend of Denver's inner-city Catholic high schools closing or relocating.

In 2006–07, Arrupe expected to serve about 270 students, 90 percent of them Hispanic, and to graduate its first class. O'Hagan assumed that all seniors would be admitted to college. Arrupe was the dream of local community leaders, many of them alums of Jesuit-run Regis High School and Regis University in the Denver area, who believed it was important to keep inner-city Catholic education alive. They formed an "extraordinary partnership" with local Jesuits and the Missouri Province to do so.

When O'Hagan recruited the school's first students using a videotape describing the success of Chicago's Cristo Rey High School, he wasn't even sure where the new school would be located. Plans "came together" when the archdiocese announced the closing of Holy Family Grade School and Middle School in northwest Denver and made the building available. A $1.7 million renovation has added science and computer labs, classrooms, and office space.

With the location secured, the second task was to find jobs for students to share. Arrupe officials had to persuade employers to hire freshmen for a collective nineteen thousand dollars a year for entry-level jobs such as filing and running errands, sometimes referring them to Cristo Rey sponsors in Chicago for reassurance that the idea works. By the fall of 2006, Arrupe had acquired sixty-five corporate partners for its work-study program, including "every major law firm and every major hospital" in the city, O'Hagan says. "We found companies that were good fits for the kids. . . . [They] are doing real work. This is not charitable compensation." More than sixty Arrupe students were working for their employers during the summer.

"We tell the kids, 'You have an eighth-grade diploma; don't overestimate your worth,'" O'Hagan says. "'You will be doing every job that no one else in the building wants to do.'"

Although Arrupe has never asked employers to mentor students, it happens naturally as work relationships develop. All the school has requested is that employers treat students as real employees. Most of the students receive excellent performance evaluations. Numerous employers have called the school to praise the students they employ.

O'Hagan says that the success of Cristo Rey schools demonstrates that what low-income students need most is the opportunity to succeed.

"To be successful, you have to know the students as people and know their families," he says. School officials must understand the obstacles that poverty creates for young people. Some of these are surfacing as Arrupe's first seniors begin to apply for college. Tough kids from tough neighborhoods are intimidated by the prospect. They look at college brochures of tree-shaded campuses filled with white faces and fear that they don't belong. All Arrupe seniors are required to apply to three colleges, and O'Hagan was optimistic that many would receive the scholarships they need to enroll.

Verbum Dei High School, Los Angeles. The Jesuits didn't start Verbum Dei, an all-male school with 340 students in the Watts area of Los Angeles. It opened in 1962 under the auspices of the Archdiocese of Los Angeles and the Society of the Divine Word Missionaries to provide low-income students with a college preparatory education. However, the school declined as its sponsoring religious order lost members.

In 2000, Verbum Dei adopted the Cristo Rey model as part of an overall effort to rebuild. Cardinal Roger Mahoney asked the Jesuits to intervene to help keep the school alive. Now the school is cosponsored by the California Province of the Jesuits and the Archdiocese of Los Angeles and is on track to eventually reach 450 students.

Verbum Dei provides transportation to and from work sites and prepares students for their jobs with classes in computing and workplace etiquette. The school's success is gaining national attention.

Related efforts. In 2006, a Jesuit-run Cristo Rey school opened in Sacramento, California, and more were in the planning stages in Minneapolis, Baltimore, and other cities. Loyola High School in Detroit is a small school for inner-city boys from poor families that has adapted the Cristo Rey concept for upperclassmen. In addition, several high schools, such as the University of Detroit Jesuit High School and McQuaid Jesuit High School, in Rochester, New York, have started academies for junior high students from inner-city areas to prepare them for a Jesuit high school education. Regis High School in New York operates the REACH program to prepare such students to compete for admission to its highly selective freshman class or scholarships to other area Catholic high schools. Numerous Nativity middle schools also work with inner-city children.

Jesuit-run Cristo Rey schools may appear to be different from traditional Jesuit schools, but they share a common Ignatian spirituality and aspirations for excellence.

"It's easy to focus on the differences, but I think these schools are so much alike in the spirit of the schools," says O'Hagan. "That's what makes Jesuit education unique. The spirit that flows through these places is so similar."

A Girl Named Micaela

When Micaela came to Arrupe Jesuit High School as a freshman, faculty members noticed how quiet she was. Her mother, who never missed a school event, spoke mostly Spanish and was obviously dedicated to helping her daughter succeed.

Had Micaela gone to a neighborhood public school with thirty-five students per class, she might have been overlooked, but in Arrupe's nurturing environment, she flourished. Her grades were excellent. She broke out of her shell to play soccer and get involved in community service. She became a class leader.

As a sophomore, she went to visit relatives in Chicago and planned a special stop—at Cristo Rey Jesuit High School. She wanted to visit the school that had inspired Arrupe's creation. She made all the arrangements herself and impressed Cristo Rey faculty so much that they always ask about her when talking to colleagues at Arrupe.

Micaela already has her college dream: to attend Loyola University Chicago, near her family and the school that indirectly gave her new life.

Micaela came to Arrupe because her mother, like most of the students' parents, trusted the school to give her a chance, says principal Michael O'Hagan.

"We don't have gang kids, but they're at a time when they have to make a choice between gangs and a much more meaningful life. Our kids have great homes. They just need the opportunity."

8

Four Urban Schools

....

I see our location as an advantage. Kids break out of their comfort zones. They get social benefits from meeting people from all backgrounds. This is a selling point to parents who realize what kind of world their kids will live in.

Dan Quesnell, class of '93,
director of communications and planning,
Marquette University High School

What do you do if you are a school in an urban neighborhood where crime is rising, housing is deteriorating, enrollment is falling, and parents and alums are urging you to either close or move to suburbia? If you're a Jesuit school committed to "faith that does justice" and "solidarity for and with the poor," the first step is to pray to discern God's will. Then you commit to staying. Instead of walling your students off in an island of privilege, you get involved in your area.

That's what several urban Jesuit high schools are doing. This is a look at University of Detroit Jesuit High School; Gonzaga College High School, in Washington, DC; Marquette University High School, in Milwaukee; and St. Ignatius High School in Cleveland. Today, all are thriving in their urban neighborhoods. Enrollments are at capacity with waiting lists and competition for seats. Multimillion-dollar capital campaigns are in progress. Neighborhood groups are using school facilities; students are reaching out through service programs. In the process, they are broadening their horizons.

University of Detroit
Jesuit High School and Academy

In the mid-1970s, Detroit was hit by the nation's worst white flight from a deteriorating central city. Unemployment and crime soared as the automotive industry declined. Detroit became a poster child for the Rust Belt. The victims of this deterioration included the University of Detroit Jesuit High School, in northwest Detroit. The school is located in what development director Ann Steele describes as a nice, working-class neighborhood, 99 percent of whose residents are African American. However, "suburbanites consider it not so nice. Just being in the city limits of Detroit is a big deal."

Enrollment fell. Parents and alumni wanted the school to move to the suburbs, and the lay board of directors concurred. The Jesuit advisory board, however, was uncertain. In 1975, members went on a retreat to pray about the decision. They came back, exercised their veto power, and announced that the school would stay where it had always been, because its mission is to serve the city and to be accessible to young men of color as well as to whites.

Things got rough. The school was saved from bankruptcy only by a two-million-dollar bequest from an alumnus. Looking for ways to boost enrollment, the school started an academy for junior high boys to prepare them for the rigors of a Jesuit high school. "We never lowered our standards," says Steele, wife of an alum and mother of a student. Instead, Detroit Jesuit helped students meet its standards by starting a tutorial program that assists students who need to catch up or who have learning disabilities. Gradually, things improved.

Today the high school has about 750 students, and the academy enrolls about 120 seventh and eighth graders. A third are minority students, and almost a third are non-Catholic. Students come from over seventy metro area communities, although the largest single group comes from near the school. A financial aid program that awards one million dollars a year promotes socioeconomic diversity.

Neighbors often use the school's running track and hold neighborhood meetings at the school. A large Baptist church uses the school's parking lots on Sundays and other occasions, Steele says. "We are the heart of the community."

School service programs like Focus: HOPE sponsor food drives, freshman service days, holiday adopt-a-family programs, and the like. There's a Christian Service Team, a core group that plans events to help all students become "men for others." All seniors do service on Wednesday mornings as a graduation requirement.

Detroit Jesuit has flourished as most of Detroit's inner-city Catholic high schools and about half of its urban Catholic elementary schools have closed because of financial problems. The campus is getting a twenty-five-million-dollar upgrade. Its future is bright.

"The reason we are in no danger is that we have incredibly loyal and generous alums," Steele says. "They credit Jesuit with their success. They are grateful to the school, and they give back."

Gonzaga College High School

After Dr. Martin Luther King Jr. was assassinated, in 1968, rioting broke out in Gonzaga College High School's historic inner-city neighborhood near the U.S. Capitol. Fires burned within a mile of the site the school has occupied since 1871. The impact was severe. Enrollment dropped from seven hundred to four hundred. The situation was exacerbated by falling numbers of Jesuits and their replacement with higher-paid lay teachers. The situation was grim. There was even talk of closing the school or moving it. A delegation of parents and alums begged the Maryland Province to keep the school open in its existing location.

Heartened by this lay support and dedicated to Gonzaga's mission, the provincial increased the Jesuit commitment to the school. Not only would Gonzaga stay open, but it would also come back stronger than ever. The school purchased land from the city for a football field and built a new gym.

Today, Gonzaga enables its neighbors to use its facilities, especially the athletic facilities. On a day in mid-June, a large group of boys attended a basketball clinic at the school. Other groups that regularly use the school include the Boys and Girls Club and the Special Olympics. Neighborhood groups that are always looking for meeting spaces find them at Gonzaga, says Fr. Allen Novotny, SJ, president.

Gonzaga reaches out in other ways. It sponsors Campus Kitchen, a program started at colleges to combat hunger. Students collect surplus food and prepare meals that they deliver to low-income neighborhood families and senior citizens. Other service efforts include tutoring inner-city children, counseling at city summer day camps, and helping at the McKenna Center for the homeless, on Gonzaga's campus. The school also sponsors programs in the Dominican Republic, weekend projects in Appalachia, and work-study programs/cultural exchanges at Red Cloud High School, in Pine Ridge, South Dakota. The annual holiday basketball tournament sponsored by the Gonzaga Fathers' Club raises funds for service programs.

Novotny says that Gonzaga is involved in helping develop the city's master plan for the neighborhood. "This is an anchor for this neighborhood. It gets us a place at the table. They respect that we stayed and are involved in the neighborhood."

Gonzaga continues to renovate its historic campus. Enrollment has grown to more than nine hundred students from all over the metropolitan area. There is stiff competition for those seats.

Marquette University High School

Marquette University High School faced its location dilemma later than University of Detroit Jesuit High School and Gonzaga College High School did. The Merrill Park neighborhood, where Marquette University High School has been located since 1925, began declining in the late 1980s. Home ownership fell. Crime rose. Gang and drug problems grew.

The neighborhood problems hurt Marquette University High School. Enrollment dropped to around 800 boys, compared with today's all-time high of 1,060. The school considered ways to boost enrollment, including moving and going coed. However, in 1990, it decided to remain all-male and in its current location.

Having committed to staying, the school took several important steps. It invested in major campus renovations, formed a partnership with the Merrill Park Neighborhood Association, and created an unarmed security force of retired Milwaukee police officers who patrol the grounds and staff a security desk at the main entrance. They wear Marquette High shirts, not police uniforms, but their presence enhances safety.

"Parents are not as fearful," says Dan Quesnell, class of '93, director of communications and planning. "We haven't had any major problems."

MUHS and the Merrill Park Neighborhood Association have collaborated on programs to revitalize the neighborhood. Between 1990 and 2002, home ownership rose from 19 percent to 60 percent, and crime dropped by 53 percent. MUHS parents and alums have invested numerous hours in the Partners Project, which rehabilitates homes in the neighborhood in order to promote home ownership.

MUHS is involved in the community in a number of other ways. The local alderman holds community meetings at the school, and the neighborhood association holds its Christmas party there. Students participate in neighborhood cleanup projects and volunteer at nearby St. Rose Catholic Urban Academy. Projects for the Christian discipleship course address a community need and often benefit the neighborhood.

Quesnell says that Marquette University High School's decision to remain in its racially diverse, blue-collar area was driven by its Ignatian mission to be in solidarity with those in need. The school is proud that about 20 percent of its students are minorities, the highest minority enrollment in its history. Close to 30 percent of the students receive financial aid worth more than $1.1 million a year.

"We could have been one of those organizations that fled this area, but we know what would have happened. Given our mission, it is best to be centrally located in Milwaukee," Quesnell says. "We are committed to being a part of our neighborhood."

St. Ignatius High School

St. Ignatius High School is located on the near West Side of Cleveland between two neighborhoods—one economically depressed, the other in the process of being gentrified by young professionals. This was once Cleveland's traditional ethnic region, with twenty Catholic churches of different backgrounds in a three-mile area. In the 1980s,

St. Ignatius High School expressed interest in purchasing more land in Ohio City, its neighborhood in Cleveland, to expand its campus with athletic fields and parking. This led some landlords to quickly sell properties to the school, displacing families. The publicity surrounding this transaction portrayed St. Ignatius High School as mistreating the neighborhood.

Partially to repair neighborhood relations, the school established the Arrupe Neighborhood Partnership in 1990, a program that involves students and alumni in renovating homes. Today, the Arrupe Neighborhood Partnership Program has moved from damage control to empowering area residents, especially young people, to change their lives by making good choices, says Tim Grady, class of '95, director of the program.

The partnership is inspired by Fr. Pedro Arrupe, SJ, who urged solidarity with the poor as a way to challenge the social conditions that make people poor. "We are not a social service agency," says Grady. "We have an endless supply of high school students who are willing to serve. Our calling card is these high school kids."

About a fourth of the fourteen hundred St. Ignatius students work with children and young teens in an after-school program that offers tutoring, sports, and field trips. The students become mentors and role models. They commit to working with an individual child for at least eight weeks in order to form a relationship with the child. Nearly one hundred students staff a five-week summer day camp that serves close to two hundred third through eighth graders.

"This is a core part of our Ignatian mission," Grady says. "Service is tied to the call of our faith. We tell students to make it a habit. It's part of our faith, not just a civic duty. We make kids believe that they have unlimited potential, which no one has told them. We call it the power of choice."

Arrupe Partnership volunteers and staff help neighborhood youth apply to Catholic high schools and apply for financial aid. They also respond to emergencies, such as power shutoffs.

The school's outreach to the poor doesn't stop there. Students and faculty meet at school on Sunday evenings to go out to distribute food to and visit with homeless people who are living under bridges in the city. They form friendships that are not "condescending," Grady says. When these homeless people walk by the school, they smile and say hi to their friends—friends with whom they have shared the stories of their lives. The school also runs the St. Joseph of Arimathea Society, which provides pallbearers for the funeral services of people who die without friends and relatives.

"I see miracles happening a lot," says Grady. "What could be a gated community for privileged young people has become a very human place."

9

Red Cloud High School

For any measure of success I have achieved, I owe much to my education at Holy Rosary Mission, which is now the Red Cloud Indian School.

Charles E. Trimble, class of '52,

Holy Rosary Mission School

Long before you could see the dancers in their colorful Lakota attire, you could hear the rhythmic pounding of the drums and the haunting sounds of chanting resounding through the prairie night. Outside the gymnasium, teens, many in Red Cloud High School sweatshirts, socialized with their friends during interludes in the dancing.

Everyone at Red Cloud High School had talked about the powwow all day. By noon, about a third of the 217 students and several teachers had departed for it. In a music class, Amery Brave Heart, class of '03, a student at Oglala Lakota College, had led a circle of boys sitting around a single large drum in singing powwow songs and pounding the drum in rhythm—the heartbeat of the Lakota nation. Two girls had stood to the side singing but not drumming, as Lakota tradition dictates.

Red Cloud High School, located in southwest South Dakota and in one of the nation's poorest counties, is an oasis on this reservation the size of Rhode Island. It is worlds away from traditional urban Jesuit prep schools literally and figuratively yet similar to them in critical ways.

Red Cloud offers students the reservation's best education, sending many to college, which wasn't even a dream twenty years ago, says Fr. Ray Bucko, SJ, professor of anthropology at Creighton University and a member of Red Cloud's board of directors. Bucko (St. Peter's Preparatory School, class of '72) taught at the school as a Scholastic from 1978 to 1980.

"The kids who come here to school find a community of sincere caring," says Fr. Peter Klink, SJ, president. "It is faith that allows our hope to never give up. We take their futures seriously."

The Jesuits have been educating the children of the Pine Ridge Reservation since 1888, when Chief Red Cloud petitioned the U.S. government to allow the "Blackrobes" to build a school. Lakota men and women helped the Jesuits build the original school from bricks formed from the clay of a nearby creek bed.

Jesuits have called teaching at Red Cloud and other Indian schools a life-changing experience, and some, like Fr. Don Doll, SJ, a photography professor at Creighton, have stayed involved with the Lakota people. Doll got his first experience in photography while teaching at St. Francis Indian School. He frequently gifts his photographs to projects that assist Red Cloud. He has received international acclaim for his books, such as *Vision Quest*, that portray Lakota life and people.

Welcome to Red Cloud

Red Cloud High School is Lakota and proud of it. Native American art and images fill its classrooms and halls. Theology classes present both Catholic beliefs and Lakota spiritual traditions. Lakota studies courses are required, and Lakota is the school's most popular "foreign language." At nearby Holy Rosary Mission Church, the stations of the cross depict Jesus as a Native American and the Roman soldiers as U.S. cavalrymen. Red Cloud art students helped design the award-winning Lakota-themed stained-glass windows.

"Our students have to be proud of themselves and proud of where they come from," says Klink, who has spent much of his Jesuit career at the school. "They need to be strong in themselves."

Red Cloud charges only a small fee and requires no uniform or dress code because of the cost. The school is funded primarily by national direct-mail solicitations, often including Doll's photographs of students in their traditional Lakota dance attire (which are also featured in Red Cloud's annual calendar). Some other Jesuit schools nationwide support Red Cloud.

One difficult task is getting students to school. Red Cloud's twenty buses travel about sixteen hundred miles a week throughout the reservation, says PR director Tina Merdanian, class of '90. Even so, many students have to walk several miles to pickup points on the main roads because their families don't have cars. Another difficulty is hiring and retaining faculty in this sparsely populated area. Many teachers, such as student activities director Nancy Kelsey, are volunteers who spend two to three years after college at Red Cloud. They come from all over the United States and live on campus.

Kelsey, a Native American from Ohio, joined Red Cloud after graduating from Creighton University. She oversees student clubs, teaches classes in creative writing and journalism, and supervises the *Red Cloud Times* student newspaper. She also runs an after-school program that combines study hall and club meetings. A special bus drives participants home. Volunteers at the school are essential and dedicated, Kelsey says, but the heavy reliance on them makes educational continuity difficult, because they change frequently.

Bucko praises Fr. Paul Coelho, SJ, principal, for enhancing the school academically. It is a far cry from the Red Cloud of the 1970s, when Bucko had "three principals in one year" and received little "direction on how to teach." Red Cloud has upgraded its technology with an excellent computer graphics lab. It has a partnership with NASA, and its students have taken top honors at the National Science Fair.

However, it is still "trying to define itself and to serve different needs," since not all students go to college, Bucko says. In addition to its academic and financial challenges, the school still must combat traditional reservation fears that it is inculcating an alien culture and values.

Balancing Ignatian and Lakota Spirituality

Red Cloud's spirituality encompasses its two worlds: Jesuit and Lakota. "On the Pine Ridge, there is not as much emphasis on what people believe as *that* they believe," says Bucko. "The Lakota culture and religion is never exclusive. There's a willingness to be compatible with lots of conflicting views. Red Cloud has to mirror the culture around it. It teaches kids to be bicultural."

Klink says Red Cloud seeks to help students understand the way that Lakota and Catholic/Jesuit spirituality mesh. "Both are life enhancing and life affirming. They enrich one another. That's how we approach it here." Red Cloud tries to be sensitive to its dual nature "to allow for both traditions to meet honestly and with integrity," he says. "These kids live in a tension. The integrity with which they live their spirituality makes them who they are."

Red Cloud High School requires four years of theology and incorporates both Catholic/Christian and Lakota elements, says Fr. Mark Carr, SJ, director of campus ministry. Alvin Slow Bear, who practices

Lakota spirituality, helps teach that tradition. The student body's religious composition is mixed. About a third of Carr's freshmen said they were Catholic or Lakota Catholic; others were non-Catholic Christian or believed in Lakota spiritual traditions. Required class retreats at a Methodist center in the Black Hills sometimes include a Mass or a Lakota prayer service, Carr says. Optional student Masses draw some students, but "it's a balancing act."

Merdanian, a Lakota Catholic, notes that Lakota people remember the years when mission schools did not allow them to practice their spirituality or culture, but now Red Cloud encourages students to "take the best of both worlds."

"For Lakota people, it is the square versus the circle," she says. The dominant American culture places things in "boxes" that proclaim the rules and how to practice them, while the Lakota culture is more flexible and adaptive.

"What has made the Jesuits so successful with the Lakota is that they are not trying to superimpose a cultural belief on our people," she says. "They allow our culture to be part of the church." For example, the reconciliation room at Holy Rosary Mission Church is built in a circle to mirror a sweat lodge.

Student and alum comments reflect ambivalence about Red Cloud's Catholic spirituality.

"At Red Cloud, you get to practice your own culture and to participate in your own Lakota spirituality," says Amery Brave Heart, the music teacher. "I grew up going to church and with Lakota spirituality. I don't much believe in the Catholic Church. I respect it, but I don't necessarily believe in it."

"I practice Lakota spirituality," says Gary Richards, class of '06. "I don't consider myself a Catholic. They require us to take theology classes. I cope with the disagreements."

Profile: Roger White Eyes

Roger White Eyes stood in the middle of his Lakota studies class wearing a T-shirt that read "Homeland Security Little Bighorn Veterans of Fighting Terrorism," casually monitoring students researching the Indian wars. "We're studying the period 1851 to 1868 that will end up with the 1868 treaty," he said. "We have a whole class on the Indian wars. All that a lot of our students know about is Wounded Knee and Little Bighorn." The course covers other clashes seldom mentioned in traditional history courses, such as the Battle of One Hundred Slain. The classroom is a mini-museum of Native American art and politics. A poster depicts sports pennants for "Negroes," "Jews," "San Diego Caucasians," and, finally, "Cleveland Indians."

White Eyes, class of '79, director of Red Cloud's Lakota studies program, says he tries "to teach the students the importance of their own history and culture from a Lakota perspective." He integrates spirituality with history, culture, and language in the required course. A native of the reservation, White Eyes was baptized and confirmed Catholic but was married by a justice of the peace. Later, he and his wife had their marriage blessed in the church. "I was one of the young radicals that really cut down the Catholic Church" for its role in the assimilation process, he says. Ironically, he returned to the church through Lakota spirituality after realizing that he was comfortable praying "both ways," in a sweat lodge and at Mass.

White Eyes received an associate degree in construction technology and worked in construction before returning to Black Hills State University, in Spearfish, South Dakota, to finish a degree in education. He student taught at Red Cloud and then accepted his current position.

White Eyes says there's still some tension between Red Cloud High School and reservation residents who believe that Lakota and Catholic culture and spirituality cannot be integrated, but "no one at school feels that way." He feels that Red Cloud's emphasis on Lakota culture and spirituality and its strong academics make it superior to Bureau of Indian Affairs public schools.

Red Cloud students "are allowed to practice their spirituality and learn about it freely without worrying about getting sued," he says. "Every day, they pray in school. They can pray in our sweat lodge."

A Gift to the Jesuits

Red Cloud has been a "gift" to Jesuits who staff it, "because we are there accompanying the Native American people in their struggle," says Doll. "If you want to find God, work with the poor, because God is with the poor."

Doll began his photography career almost accidentally while teaching on the reservation at a Jesuit school, by taking pictures when someone asked if he could use a camera. He also found that he could teach and coach. "I discovered some talents that I didn't think I had. [I] began listening to that inner voice. Really it was the Holy Spirit speaking in [me]. Maybe that would have happened anyhow, but I doubt it."

His Marquette University High School classmate (class of '55) Fr. Richard Hauser, SJ, a professor of theology at Creighton University, says he too was profoundly affected by his year of teaching on a reservation. He says that the hardships of reservation life and the frustrations of his job forced him to turn to God for the affirmation he wasn't getting from people. He recalls taking long walks at night and praying. Before, he had thought of prayer as something done in church, not as a relationship with God.

"I developed a whole understanding of prayer that I hadn't had before," says Hauser.

Bucko says the Lakota people taught him the importance of remaining integrated with his family—sometimes a challenge for Jesuits who live and work far from home. "If the Lakota do anything, it is care for their families. There is always mutual support and a willingness to work together, while in our own culture we tend to be self-actualizing."

Bucko has been adopted by several Lakota families and has brought his family to the reservation. Lakota culture includes an adoption ritual in which outsiders become members of their new families, a relationship that both sides take very seriously.

Profile: Charles E. Trimble

Before Red Cloud High School, there was Holy Rosary Mission School, a Jesuit-run boarding school that mirrored the Bureau of Indian Affairs boarding schools in which generations of Native American children were educated.

Charles Trimble, class of '52 at Holy Rosary, reflected on his experiences there years later, assessing the criticism such schools have received. He is a former executive director of the National Congress of American Indians and the principal founder of the American Indian Press Association.

Here are excerpts from his column in Indian Country Today *on his alma mater:*

It was back in 1971, and several of us were sitting around a bar table trying to out-Indian each other. The competition was who had it roughest in boarding school. . . . The gist . . . is how we viewed our boarding school experience—as a challenge met and endured, and to be boasted about. . . .

My father died in 1937, leaving my mother alone to raise five boys. . . . Two years later, with the threat of losing me to adoption as social workers were insisting, my mother decided instead to place me in a Catholic mission school, even though I was only four years old at the time.

It was to be the first time I would be away from home for an extended period, and I dreaded it. My brother, slightly older, would be there with me, but that was little comfort to me. While my mother enrolled us, I stayed close to her side. But my brother lured me into the playroom to see a special toy or game. . . . I sensed that something was terribly wrong. . . . Tearing back outside, I saw that my mother was gone. . . . Thus began my school days at Holy Rosary Mission in Pine Ridge, South Dakota. . . .

I spent the rest of my school years at the mission, graduating in 1952. Over those years I met good people—teachers, administrators, and fellow students. . . .

Life would have been better if I could have stayed in Wanblee with my mother and brothers in our home, which was very poor in material goods, but rich with love and affection. Looking back now, I see Wanblee as always Christmas or summertime, for those were the only times I spent there during my growing-up years. . . . If the mission meant to kill the Indian in me—and I don't believe that was their intent—it would have been futile anyway, given the fullness and richness of my cultural world at Wanblee, even in those few months I spent at home each year.

Life in the school was often very hard, especially for the little ones. . . . Discipline was strict and spanking was not uncommon. . . . In the crowded dormitories, disease, such as measles and whooping cough, spread rapidly and laid up many students at any time. But, as with children everywhere, there was also warm friendship, joy and laughter, adventure, and much mischief. . . .

And life was frustrating for adolescents. . . . Classes were coeducational through the fifth grade; from there on, the gender separation was complete. . . . Except on Sunday afternoons and at Sodality dances, there was never a chance to even hold hands. . . .

I was a problem to most of the teachers and was sent many times to the principal's office. A demerit system was in place, with the worst punishment being study hall instead of the movie on Saturday night. I missed many movies and spent much time struggling to write the required five-hundred-word compositions while listening to the laughter and clapping in the gymnasium above, where the movies were shown. On one occasion I was nearly expelled, saved only by my mother's intercession.

I learned to survive, however, and am proud of the fact that I finished school there. . . .

I witnessed and experienced spankings, but nothing that could be described as beatings.

I remember no prohibition, written or otherwise, on speaking the Lakota language. And if there was, signals were certainly confusing, for there were prayers and songs in Lakota. Student dancers performed in full regalia before each basketball game, and there were cheers in Lakota during the games. To refine his newly acquired language, Jesuit Scholastic John Bryde regaled young students with the *Aeneid*, much improvised and in Lakota.

This is not to deny the hardship that existed in the lonesomeness, strict discipline, and the constant survival struggle in the boarding schools. But by the time I graduated, conditions were much improved over what they were when I first started. Daily

Mass was no longer mandatory, for example, and students were allowed to go home on weekends. A decade after I graduated, Indian studies was incorporated into the curriculum, including Lakota language. . . .

My greatest motivation for toughing it out was the fact that the person who placed me in the school and kept me there was the one who loved me the most and cared the most about my future. That, of course, was my Lakota mother. Knowing that, I was able to endure.

I have no regrets. For any measure of success I have achieved, I owe much to my education at Holy Rosary Mission, which is now the Red Cloud Indian School.

10

Two Schools Linked by Katrina

I was awestruck by this whole thing. The Jesuits have a philosophy of men for others, but they don't just say it—they live it.

Kathleen Juhas, assistant principal for academics,

Jesuit High School, New Orleans

Darkness had fallen over Houston hours ago on this November evening in 2005, but Strake Jesuit College Preparatory School's campus was all lit up. Recently installed floodlights even illuminated an intramural sports field outside the cafeteria. In the theology class of Br. Larry Huck, SJ, it was business as usual.

Or was it? The sweatshirts said New Orleans Jesuit or Blue Jays, not Strake Jesuit Crusaders. Students had eaten dinner, not lunch, in the cafeteria. Most would go home to host families, not their parents. Fr. Mark Thibodeaux, SJ, pastoral minister at Strake Jesuit, saw only unfamiliar faces when he roved the hallways. Those students were counting the days until Thanksgiving break, longing for what they would not find—"New Orleans as it was before Katrina," as one senior said.

In late August of 2005, Hurricane Katrina had flooded New Orleans Jesuit, destroying eleven classrooms, eight offices, and the switchboard. The recently renovated auditorium was ruined. All cafeteria equipment was destroyed, along with portions of the heating and air-conditioning system. The new student commons was gutted. There was heavy damage to the Louis J. Roussel Jr. physical education building and roof damage to the Chapel of the North American Martyrs.

The New Orleans Jesuit students had to go elsewhere or lose a semester. As a result, they became the grateful beneficiaries of a remarkable joint effort of Strake Jesuit College Prep and thirty-four of their own faculty members: a Sunday-to-Thursday evening "school within a school" that served at its peak more than four hundred displaced youths.

For Strake Jesuit, it meant creating the parallel high school program in a matter of days and sharing its facilities with others. For New Orleans Jesuit faculty, it meant teaching in Houston for a semester, often separated from their families and having to delay rebuilding their own lives. Strake Jesuit families housed many of the New Orleans students and teachers.

"I was awestruck by this whole thing," says Kathleen Juhas, New Orleans Jesuit's assistant principal for academics, who supervised the program. "The Jesuits have a philosophy of men for others, but they don't just say it—they live it."

"This is unprecedented, to my knowledge," said Gavin Atilano, a New Orleans Jesuit senior.

Responding to the Emergency

When Hurricane Katrina hit, Strake Jesuit was already at capacity with 870 students and had a freshman waiting list. Then the heartbreaking calls started coming in to the admissions office. Soon there were fifty, then over ninety. The pleas for help just kept coming. "We started talking about what if we couldn't just fit the students in," says Fr. Daniel Lahart, SJ, president. Strake Jesuit had rented buildings in anticipation of accommodating some transfer students. There was even talk of letting students sit on the floor if need be.

By the end of the week that Katrina struck, Strake Jesuit faced serving more than two hundred New Orleans students; numbers continued to grow, especially after New Orleans Jesuit's Web site announced that Strake Jesuit would accept hurricane transfers. Students e-mailed scattered friends about their plans to attend Strake Jesuit, attracting still more applicants.

The entire Strake Jesuit community mobilized behind the effort. LeeAnn Badum, a Mothers' Club board member, helped handle admissions calls. "It was heartrending to talk to those families," she says. "Their homes were gone. They didn't know what to do with their kids." The Mothers' Club organized a clothing drive and helped with a special registration day for the New Orleans students. They registered 265 boys on the Tuesday after the hurricane hit, she says.

Badum, a nurse, also helped with admissions physicals, which demonstrated the stress that students were feeling. Before taking the boys' blood pressure, medical volunteers tried to calm them down, especially the seniors, who best understood what was happening.

"The parents registered the kids, and many had to leave them," she says. "One mother burst into tears and said, 'I am out of money, and I don't know where we'll sleep or what to do.' The mother at the registration table said, 'You'll stay with me' and took her and her family home."

Tuition for the emergency program was free, although Strake Jesuit accepted contributions from around the nation to defray costs.

The Badum Family Expands

While not all host family placements worked well, Badum and her husband, Jim, happily expanded their family circle to include Jeff Guilbeau—a freshman, like their son, Michael—and a group of Jeff's friends.

Jim Badum would pick up Jeff and his friends when they got out of school, around 9:00 p.m. One night as he drove, he questioned the boys about how school had gone and kidded them about their successes or failures on tests and assignments. Just as their fathers would have, he asked them how Latin had gone. Was the science quiz hard? Thursday evenings brought brownies and ice cream at the Badum home to celebrate the end of the school week.

The Badums assigned chores to the New Orleans boys to make them feel at home. LeeAnn Badum also encouraged Jeff and his friends to attend Strake Jesuit social activities, such as homecoming. She helped set them up with dates for the dance.

The Badum children, Michael and five-year-old Annie, and Jeff became close. Michael began doing his homework earlier so he could socialize with his new friends after they got out of school. Annie called Jeff her new brother and said she wished he didn't have to leave. Jeff's friend Malcolm Andry spent most mornings and afternoons at the Badum home.

"There's nothing bad about this. It's been fun," said Michael.

"I'd love to have Michael live with me," added Malcolm.

"I think God's hand is in this," said LeeAnn Badum.

Giving Thanks, Giving Back

Several New Orleans Jesuit students expressed their gratitude to Strake Jesuit and said they have a greatly enhanced understanding of the meaning of "men for others."

"Houston in general and Strake Jesuit have been so warm and inviting," said senior Gavin Atilano. "The administration had its ducks in order. They did a fine job considering the time they had. My host family are the nicest people I've ever met."

"This has been the best we could hope for, given the situation," said Paul Loeb, also a senior.

Despite the difficulties, New Orleans Jesuit carried out a beloved tradition that Thanksgiving: a food distribution program that gave scattered students a chance to reconnect. The drive was much smaller than in the past, but it drew national TV coverage.

"I've felt good doing the Thanksgiving drive every year, but it has been sort of forced," said Loeb. "This year it is different. I have a whole new outlook on charity from all that we have received. I'm upset that I can't participate. Now it's something I wish I could be in town for."

Other Jesuit Schools Also Responded

No other Jesuit school could match Strake Jesuit's response to the students displaced by Hurricane Katrina, but many reached out, especially Jesuit College Preparatory School of Dallas, which took in seventy New Orleans Jesuit transfer students. Smaller numbers of students temporarily enrolled at many other Jesuit schools throughout the country, and many schools donated to the school's Hurricane Restoration Project.

Fr. Philip Postell, SJ, president of Dallas Jesuit, says his school was able to integrate the transfer students into existing classes, and the school did not charge the transfer students tuition.

Postell, an alum of New Orleans Jesuit, compared the relief efforts to the parable of the Good Samaritan. "Who is my neighbor? Did we really have a choice as a Christian institution? We instantly said yes to about every query. The point is to serve the kids and some of the families."

New Orleans Jesuit High Reopens

On January 23, 2006, New Orleans Jesuit High opened for its second semester with 1,300 students, down only 150 from its student body at the beginning of the school year. Jesuit was the first flooded school in New Orleans to reopen, despite the fifteen million dollars in damages it suffered (to facilities and equipment). Insurance, loans, and government funds covered only part of these costs. The school conducted a massive fund drive to pay for rebuilding that drew donations from alums all over the country as well as other Jesuit schools.

PART 3

PROFILES OF ALUMNI AND SCHOOLS

11

Notable Jesuit Alumni

....

From the Jesuits I learned the imperative of giving back to
society several-fold what society and others have given to you.

—Leo Hindery, class of '65
Bellarmine Preparatory School

Bob Newhart, Comedian and Actor
St. Ignatius College Prep, Chicago, Class of '47

Legendary comedian Bob Newhart has starred in two of television
history's most popular series, won an Emmy Award, made a comic
record that outsold Elvis when it was released, and been profiled on
PBS's *American Masters*. Not bad for a guy who lived with his parents
until he was nearly thirty and worked as an accountant after graduating from St. Ignatius College Prep and Loyola University Chicago.

Newhart broke into comedy in the late 1950s when he was working as an ad copywriter for a film and TV producer. He would make
tapes of one-sided telephone conversations with historic figures, such
as Abraham Lincoln and Sir Walter Raleigh, and send them into a
local radio station that would air them. A talent scout from Warner
Bros. Records loved the bits and signed him. *The Button-Down Mind
of Bob Newhart* became the first comedy album to reach number one
on the charts.

A comic legend was born: the understated guy who is an island of sanity in an insane world. Newhart played this role in his two memorable TV series, *The Bob Newhart Show* and *Newhart*. In the first, he played a Chicago psychologist, and in the second, he played an innkeeper in Vermont. *Newhart* ended with what some have called one of the classic final episodes. He returns as his psychologist character and wakes up next to Suzanne Pleshette, his wife in *The Bob Newhart Show*. He proclaims that he has just had a dream that he was an innkeeper in Vermont.

Newhart's offscreen life is unconventional for a major star. His routines have always been notably clean, and he and his wife, Virginia, always took their four children to Mass. His sister is a nun.

Newhart's many awards include the Sword of Loyola, given by Loyola University Chicago for dedication and service in a field outside medicine. He has assisted various Jesuit institutions with fundraising. Fr. John Schlegel, SJ, president of Creighton University, calls Newhart "an icon of integrity, values, and care in the cosmetic world of Hollywood. His private and professional lifestyle speaks to his embracing of Jesuit values." Newhart's friendship with Schlegel led to Newhart's star role in a DVD promoting the university's four-hundred-million-dollar capital campaign.

Anthony Lazzara Jr., Physician and Humanitarian
Jesuit High School of Tampa, Class of '60

In 1983, Dr. Anthony Lazzara Jr. left a tenured position at Emory University School of Medicine, sold his possessions, and moved to Chaclacayo, Peru, in the foothills of the Andes, to care for destitute children. Villa la Paz, Lazzara's clinic near Lima, provides free care and medicines to children whose parents cannot afford health care.

A native of Tampa, Lazzara graduated from the Jesuit High School of Tampa; Jesuit-run Spring Hill College, in Mobile, Alabama; and Tulane University School of Medicine. He specialized in pediatrics, eventually joining the faculty of Emory University School of Medicine, in Atlanta.

His life changed when a Franciscan missionary visited his Atlanta parish and told him of the need for missionaries in third-world countries. Lazzara moved to Peru and spent four years working at a Franciscan dispensary, then purchased a house called Hogar San Francisco de Asis (St. Francis of Assisi Home) and opened his own clinic for children.

Every day, Lazzara treats about fifty children afflicted with illnesses such as tuberculosis, malnutrition, chronic diarrhea, and leukemia and with surgical conditions such as cleft palate. No patient has ever been turned away.

The clinic's Web site (www.villalapazfoundation.org) describes a typical day, beginning at 6:00 a.m. with a check on the children staying at the house, breakfast, and cleaning.

"By 8:30, I am making rounds with the nurse in charge, going over each child's chart, and receiving the report of the preceding day and night, planning what changes, if any, are needed in the care of the child." Later, Lazzara sees and admits patients. Children must be poor and too ill to be cared for at home.

Lazzara said that before coming to Peru, he felt "an unease, a feeling that I was not where I was supposed to be, that the Lord would have me elsewhere."

He and his family created the Villa la Paz Foundation to support his work. As the Web site says, "We invite you to participate with us in the care of God's forgotten little ones. We are the only hope these children have. Every dollar sent to the Foundation is used for medical care and food for the destitute."

Ed Macauley, Deacon and Basketball Hall of Famer
St. Louis University High School, Class of '45

When future NBA Hall of Famer "Easy Ed" Macauley graduated from St. Louis University High School, his mother said he could choose any college that was "Catholic and in St. Louis." He led the St. Louis University basketball team to the 1948 National Invitational Tournament championship and was named a consensus first-team all-American and an AP player of the year in 1949. He acquired his nickname his first night as team captain, when he nervously dashed onto the court, wondering why no one followed before realizing that the national anthem was playing. "Take it easy, Ed," fans yelled.

After college, Macauley starred for the Boston Celtics and the St. Louis Hawks. He later coached the Hawks and served as sports director for two television stations in St. Louis before his final retirement. He was a seven-time NBA all-star, scored 11,234 points in 641 games (17.5 ppg), and led the Hawks to an NBA championship as a player and to two Western Division championships as a coach. In 1990, he was named one of basketball's one hundred greatest players.

Macauley was ordained a Catholic deacon in 1989 and coauthored the book *Homilies Alive*. He has conducted workshops on giving effective homilies and works with the Web site Homiliesalive.com, which provides priests and deacons with free assistance in developing homilies by providing sample homilies for specific weeks in both Spanish and English. It also includes links to books and other resources.

Macauley calls St. Louis University High School "the perfect boys' high school. The faculty developed the idea that we could all be whatever we wanted to be. As a sophomore, I was the substitute center on the 'B' team and didn't play much. However, the discipline I learned there helped me to continue practicing by myself. It paid off. They taught us the importance of our faith and the importance of family." Macauley's two sons and three of his grandsons also graduated from St. Louis University High. One of his grandsons attended the school's "archrival," De Smet High School, and Macauley kiddingly concludes that it must be improving.

Fr. Greg Boyle, SJ, Minister to Gang Members
Loyola High School of Los Angeles, Class of '72

Fr. Greg Boyle, SJ, of Los Angeles, has gained international recognition for combating gang violence in East Los Angeles. Boyle is the founder of Jobs for a Future and Homeboy Industries, organizations that help young people make the transition from gangs to jobs. Few Jesuits have ever picked a tougher crowd to minister to.

The Jesuits of Loyola High School fostered Boyle's vocation. In Celeste Fremon's book about Boyle, *Father Greg and the Homeboys*, she says that he saw them as "not only inspiring and cutting-edge but as genuinely happy when happiness seemed to him to be a foreign and rare commodity among adults." When he graduated from Loyola High, he told his parents he was joining the Jesuits.

An early assignment to the Christian base communities in Cochabamba, Bolivia, introduced him to the satisfactions of working with the poor. In 1986, he became pastor of Dolores Mission Parish, the poorest parish in the Los Angeles Archdiocese. Here he began working with gang members. He created Jobs for a Future to combat gang violence. It in turn led to the creation of Homeboy Industries.

Jobs for a Future coaches young people in job readiness, interview skills, and résumé preparation and teaches youth how to dress for work. It also offers free tattoo removal, because tattoos can hurt employment prospects. The organization acts as a free employment referral center for employers and monitors the progress of the young people it places.

Homeboy Industries, founded in 1992, is the economic development branch of Jobs for a Future. It includes five small businesses staffed by former gang members who provide cleaning services and produce baked goods, apparel, and merchandise with the Homeboy logo. Two principles guide these organizations: "Nothing Stops a Bullet Like a Job" and "Jobs, not Jails." Boyle often attacks society's failure to treat gang members as human beings who need love and help.

Boyle, whom "homeboys" often call "G Dog," "G," or just Fr. Greg, has been profiled not only in Fremon's book but also in numerous articles. In 2003, Loyola High School presented him with its prestigious Cahalan Award.

Harry Connick Jr., Singer, Musician, and Actor
Jesuit High School, New Orleans, Class of '85

New Orleans is music, and music is New Orleans.

While it has become almost customary for celebrities to raise funds for disaster relief, it's different when the disaster hits your hometown. When Hurricane Katrina struck New Orleans, native son Harry Connick Jr. rescued victims and personalized the catastrophe for the nation, becoming an indelible part of the city's Hurricane Katrina saga.

Evening after evening, Connick, a Grammy Award–winning singer whose albums have sold more than twenty million copies, led network newscasters through the horrors of the flooded city. One segment featured him and his father, a retired district attorney and lounge singer, coming home and showing off Connick's beloved first piano, which had been damaged.

Connick, a graduate of Jesuit High School, released the song "All These People" to raise money for the New Orleans Habitat Musicians' Village, a rebuilding project that he and Branford Marsalis founded. The song, featuring singer Kim Burrell, was the first single on his *Oh, My NOLA* New Orleans big-band album. Connick and Marsalis also were honorary chairs of Habitat for Humanity's hurricane relief program.

Connick is an actor as well as a singer. In addition to his three Grammy Awards, he has won Tony and Emmy awards and has been nominated for Academy, Golden Globe, and Cable Ace awards. His albums include *Songs I Heard, Harry for the Holidays*, and *Only You*. Among his film credits are *Memphis Belle, Hope Floats*, and *Independence Day*, while his TV achievements include the ABC production of *South Pacific* and a recurring role on NBC's *Will & Grace*.

In the aftermath of the hurricane, Connick told *The Today Show* about an "incredible" sight at the St. Louis Cathedral, the oldest in the United States. "In the back, there's a courtyard, and there's a statue of Jesus with his arms outstretched. . . . And there are these huge oak trees. The root system was taller than me. And they were crashed all around the statue—I mean, inches, six inches—and the statue just remained there. And it was unbelievable to see. It was just a really nice feeling in the middle of all of this."

Kate Johnson, Olympic Medalist
Jesuit High School, Portland, Oregon, Class of '97

Kate Johnson, a member of Portland Jesuit High School's first coed class, is the school's first alum to win an Olympic medal—a silver in rowing at the 2004 Olympics. But her career is far from over.

In addition to training for the 2008 Olympics in Beijing, she volunteers for Right to Play, along with other Olympic medalists. The organization uses sports to promote health education, the importance of vaccinations, and the prevention of diseases such as HIV/AIDS, tuberculosis, and malaria in poor countries such as Ethiopia, where Johnson has worked.

Johnson visited Portland Jesuit the spring before it turned coed, trying to imagine what it would be like with girls. New to Portland that year, she also tackled a new sport, rowing, after seeing racing boats on the Willamette River. Thus began her Olympic dream.

"I was a novice and knew no limitations. My first year of rowing marks one of the purest times in my life. It was a time when anything seemed possible as long as I loved doing it. *Age quod agis*: 'Do well whatever you do.' The message is ingrained in the brain of every student who leaves Jesuit for the rest of his and her life. [When I was] a high school freshman, the words seemed daunting and ambiguous, yet over time I learned how simple and clear a message those words really were."

Johnson became an all-American in rowing at the University of Michigan, then earned the last seat in the eight-person crew for the 2004 games. In Athens, the Americans finished second to the Romanians by 1.86 seconds.

After the Olympics, Johnson took a job in the Olympics division of the IMG sports marketing firm in New York, then volunteered for Right to Play. It sent her to Ethiopia, where she told a reporter that in playing soccer with blind children, she found a reward greater than an Olympic medal.

"You think about a smile and how many impressions a smile makes. The whole point is that every kid deserves the opportunity to be just a kid."

Leo Hindery, Businessman and Philanthropist
Bellarmine Preparatory School, Tacoma, Washington, Class of '65

A man who started working at age nine to help pay for his Catholic education and later headed TCI, then the nation's largest cable television company, and Global Crossing Ltd. gave his alma mater, Bellarmine Prep, its biggest gift, $3.75 million for scholarships for at-risk youth.

"One of the many reasons I love the Jesuits is that they recognize the moral imperative of equal opportunity," said Leo Hindery, in a speech at Bellarmine Prep. He also is a former NASCAR racer, a cofounder of Transatlantic Partners against AIDS, and a columnist for *BusinessWeek* online.

He credits Bellarmine with laying the foundations for his success.

"Here I learned to read with curiosity and to express myself," he told the school. "Here I learned to work hard. Here I learned to respect others, and here, from the Jesuits, I learned the imperative of giving back to society several-fold what society and others have given to you."

Hindery graduated from Seattle University and received an MBA from Stanford University before launching his business career. Although he came from a family that "struggled more than a bit financially," he benefited from being white and male "at a time just like today, when being white and being male are economic and educational advantages."

Speaking to Bellarmine students, he said, "If you are left out of this world at any stage, but especially at the at-risk stage, you can never pedal fast enough to catch up."

Hindery, who received Bellarmine Prep's highest award, the St. Robert Bellarmine Award, has been honored internationally for fighting AIDS. His book *It Takes a CEO* challenges fellow CEOs to take responsibility for making ethical decisions. He also has been a finalist for chairman of the Democratic National Committee.

He urged Bellarmine Prep to "thank God for the education which is received here, make certain it is available to *all* the youth of Tacoma, and instill in them and yourselves the imperative of giving back to society and, in the process, to God gifts which we received."

Raul Julia, Actor
Colegio San Ignacio de Loyola, Class of '57

Raul Julia, a graduate of Colegio San Ignacio de Loyola, in San Juan, Puerto Rico, was not only a noteworthy actor but also a philanthropist who lived the Jesuit ideals he absorbed in high school by becoming a passionate supporter of the Hunger Project. For seventeen years, before his death following a stroke in 1994, he served as spokesperson for this foundation devoted to the elimination of world hunger.

Julia was born in San Juan and obtained a BA in drama from the University of Puerto Rico before moving to New York in 1964 to pursue an acting career. He appeared in more than forty-five movies and TV shows and received four Tony Award nominations. His movie credits include *Kiss of the Spider Woman, Presumed Innocent, Romero,* and *The Burning Season,* for which he received an Emmy and a Golden Globe Award (posthumously). His portrayal of the martyred archbishop Oscar Romero of El Salvador was especially strong and moving.

Julia left a lasting impact both on-screen and, possibly more important, off, through his work fighting hunger. "There are 38,000 people dying of hunger each day and most are children. And, being a celebrity, I communicate about it as much as I can," he told *Elle* magazine in 1987.

Following his death, the Raul Julia Ending Hunger Fund was established in 1994. In addition, his advocacy inspired the Hunger Project to expand its operations into Latin America in 1998.

Mildred J. Calvesbert, principal of Colegio San Ignacio, praised her noted alum: "Raul was an extraordinary human being and a wonderful family man. He never forgot his roots, and his heart went out to those in need. He truly believed that he would live to see the end of hunger in the world. He worked hard toward this goal and left a memorable legacy of people committed to the cause."

St. Louis Jesuits, Musicians

Fr. John Foley, SJ
  Chaplain Kapaun Memorial High School, Class of '57
Fr. Bob Dufford, SJ
  Creighton Preparatory School, Class of '61
Dan Schutte
  Marquette University High School, Class of '66
Fr. Robert "Roc" O'Connor, SJ
  Creighton Preparatory School, Class of '67

"Be Not Afraid," "One Bread, One Body," "Lift Up Your Hearts," "City of God"—the list goes on and on. For millions of Catholics, these hymns and others by the St. Louis Jesuits evoke memories of weddings and funerals, baptisms and first communions. Weekly liturgies everywhere are enriched by this warm, simple music grounded in Scripture. The music of the St. Louis Jesuits filled the liturgical vacuum created by the transition from Latin to English. To many Catholics, especially those who grew up in the era of the Second Vatican Council, St. Louis Jesuits music *is* church music.

All four of the primary composers—Fr. John Foley, SJ; Fr. Bob Dufford, SJ; Dan Schutte; and Fr. Roc O'Connor, SJ—are graduates of Jesuit high schools who spent their spare time during their seminary years in St. Louis in the 1970s writing contemporary hymns accompanied by guitar. People from all over the nation who heard the music at a Jesuit chapel at St. Louis University requested copies to take home. The authors supplied handwritten lyrics run off on a mimeograph machine.

In 1973, as group members were finishing their studies and leaving St. Louis, they collected their songs into a book and, almost impulsively, decided to record them. With financial support from Schutte's parents and their provinces, they recorded their first album, *Neither Silver nor Gold*, a four-record set that sold rapidly. Fr. Jack Zuercher, SJ, then formation director for the Wisconsin Province, said that the Society would support future albums.

The St. Louis Jesuits' most popular album, *Earthen Vessels*, released in 1975, has sold more than a million copies. Five more collections followed during the next decade: *A Dwelling Place, Gentle Night, Wood Hath Hope, Lord of Light*, and *The Steadfast Love*. After a twenty-year hiatus, the group reunited and released a new album, *Morning Light*, in 2005. The group's work has been translated into a dozen languages, including Russian, Croatian, and Finnish. Their hymns appear in the missals and hymnals used by 60 percent of the nation's eighteen thousand Catholic churches and numerous Protestant churches.

O'Connor, a liturgist and theology professor at Creighton University, says the seeds of his life's work were planted at Creighton Prep.

"Attending Prep made me a better human being—intellectually, socially, but above all spiritually. Whether in the classroom, on the playing field, in JUG, working on the switchboard, at Mass, in confession, or on retreat, the priests, brothers, and Scholastics at Prep influenced me enough to want to become a Jesuit. They sowed seeds of scholarship, a love of humanity, and a contemporary piety that has made all the difference in my life, bearing fruit in the years following. I am very grateful to these good men, many of whom I have ministered with over the years. I continue to be blessed by their wisdom and insight. Go Bluejays!"

Tim Russert, Journalist
Canisius High School, Class of '68

In Jesuit circles, it is a toss-up whether NBC News Washington bureau chief Tim Russert is better known for moderating *Meet the Press* and his political analysis or for his unabashed enthusiasm for his Jesuit education.

Russert grew up in blue-collar South Buffalo, the son of "Big Russ," a manager for the city's sanitation system. When his seventh-grade teacher Sr. Lucille suggested that he take the competitive test for Canisius High School, he refused, believing the school was "for rich people," as he says in his memoir, *Big Russ & Me*. Still, Sr. Lucille persuaded him to take the Canisius test, and he won a scholarship that changed his life.

"I . . . had never even considered applying; it just wasn't something that people like me did. It would be like suddenly applying to Harvard or Yale when you had spent your whole life planning to attend the nearest branch of the state university," he writes in *Big Russ & Me*.

Russert became the first member of his family to go to college. "Although I didn't realize it at the time, when I took the Canisius entrance exam and was accepted to the school, I was turning onto a big new road on which college followed high school as surely as night follows day." He received a scholarship from Jesuit-run John Carroll University, in Cleveland, from which he graduated. He earned a law degree at Cleveland State University, joined the staff of New York senator Daniel Patrick Moynihan, and later served as a counselor to New York governor Mario Cuomo.

In 1984, Russert joined NBC News as a deputy to its president. He later became head of the NBC News Washington bureau and began moderating *Meet the Press*. He also does political analysis for *Today* and *Nightly News* and hosts *Tim Russert* on CNBC. His memoir of his youth, *Big Russ & Me*, became a best seller and inspired a second book, *Wisdom of Our Fathers*.

None of this would have happened had Sr. Lucille not persuaded the bright kid from South Buffalo to apply to Canisius High School. "She put me on a path that ultimately led to far bigger opportunities than I had ever imagined for myself."

12

Profiles of Jesuit High Schools

T he March King," John Philip Sousa, at one time directed the marching band at Gonzaga College High School, in Washington, DC. One of the buildings on Chicago's St. Ignatius College Prep campus was the original site of the Field Museum of Natural History—one of the few buildings to survive the Great Chicago Fire—and still displays some natural history artifacts. Xavier High School, in New York, was a Jesuit military school and still boasts an outstanding Junior ROTC program and a nationally ranked drill team.

These bits of Jesuit high school trivia illustrate the rich heritage of individual institutions. While the schools share many similarities, it is important to spotlight each school's history and programs, at least briefly. This section presents mini-portraits of each of the forty-nine Jesuit high schools, drawn mostly from their Web sites, that suggest features that make each school special.

In 1789, John Carroll, SJ, the first bishop of the United States, founded the first Jesuit high school, Georgetown Preparatory School, the only Jesuit boarding school in the country today. Many of the schools founded before 1900 were originally part of what became separate universities, at a time when there wasn't a clear distinction between high school and college. In many cases, either the high school or the college moved to a separate location, but Fairfield College Preparatory School still shares a campus with Fairfield University.

Wealthy local donors provided funding to start many of the newer Jesuit high schools, such as New York's Regis High School, which remains tuition-free thanks to the generosity of its founding family and alums. Sometimes donors, like the Walsh family of Cuyahoga Falls, Ohio, who founded Walsh Jesuit High School, waged lengthy campaigns with church leaders and Jesuit authorities to start schools. Jesuit high school alums from the East and Midwest who moved to Houston after World War II were instrumental in starting Strake Jesuit College Preparatory. Cardinal Joseph Bernardin's request that the Jesuits serve Chicago's Hispanic community sparked the Cristo Rey movement.

Most of the traditional Jesuit schools were founded as all-male institutions, although about a third are now coed, including all but one of the Cristo Rey schools. Regis Jesuit High School, located outside Denver, has created an all-female division to complement its long-standing all-male division. Whether coed or single sex, each school I visited seemed pleased with its current status.

Loyola High School in Detroit is the smallest Jesuit high school, serving fewer than two hundred inner-city boys. Loyola Academy, in Wilmette, Illinois, is the largest, with a coed enrollment of more than two thousand. St. Xavier High School, in Cincinnati, is the nation's largest all-male high school, with fifteen hundred boys.

The following profiles highlight the history, programs, and achievements of each school. In order to keep the portraits brief, details of major academic and athletic achievements more or less common to all the schools have been left out:

- It's hard to find a Jesuit school that hasn't won some kind of state sports championship, and often many championships per year, because nearly all Jesuit high schools excel athletically.
- All Jesuit schools boast of college enrollments, outstanding academics with noteworthy SAT/ACT scores, numerous National Merit Scholars, and other academic honors.

- The schools share a commitment to service, ministry, and retreats; run strong cocurricular programs; and are successful at fund-raising.

Individual school Web sites are great sources of detailed information. The Jesuit Secondary Education Association's Web site (www.jsea .org) contains links to all the school Web sites.

Welcome to this introductory tour of the Jesuit high schools!

— IHS —

Arrupe Jesuit High School

Location: Denver, Colorado
Founded: 2003
Number of Students: 270
Student Body: Coed
Nickname: Generals

Interesting Information

Arrupe Jesuit High School, one of the schools in the Cristo Rey Network, recruited its first students before it even found a location by showing a videotape about the work-study program at Cristo Rey Jesuit High School in Chicago. Arrupe's low-income students (the vast majority of whom are Hispanic) earn about 70 percent of their tuition through a work-study program modeled on Cristo Rey's. Arrupe's opening helped counter Denver's loss of several inner-city Catholic high schools.

The school is named in honor of Fr. Pedro Arrupe, SJ, who believed that religious faith grounded in the gospel must oppose oppression and injustice, alleviate poverty, and eradicate racial discrimination. Arrupe

Jesuit High School requires all of its seniors to apply to at least three colleges and expects virtually all of them to attend college.

— IHS —

Bellarmine College Preparatory

Location: San Jose, California
Founded: 1851
Number of Students: 1,450
Student Body: All-male
Nickname: Bells

Interesting Information

Bellarmine College Preparatory School is the oldest Jesuit high school on the West Coast, founded as part of Santa Clara College. It was called Santa Clara Prep before changing its name to Bellarmine College Preparatory in 1926.

Bellarmine takes advantage of its "unique location in the heart of Silicon Valley" by providing students with an "admittedly overbuilt" technology infrastructure, which includes state-of-the-art computer facilities in every classroom. "Our goal is to identify, maintain, and implement cutting-edge personal and enterprise technologies for the sole purpose of enhancing the college preparatory learning experience a Bellarmine student receives." Teachers are expected to be proficient in new technology so that they are "more efficient in their daily duties," thus allowing them to "spend more time face-to-face with their students."

Noted Alumni

Pat Burrell, outfielder for the Philadelphia Phillies

Ming Chen, associate justice of the California Supreme Court
Erik Howard, former NFL lineman
Tom McEnery, former mayor of San Jose
Stephen Mirrione, film editor
Dan Pastorini, former NFL quarterback

— IHS —

Bellarmine Preparatory School

Location: Tacoma, Washington
Founded: 1928
Number of Students: 1,000
Student Body: Coed
Nickname: Lions

Interesting Information

Bellarmine Preparatory School occupies a forty-two-acre campus over-looking Mount Rainier and Tacoma. Originally all-male, it merged with all-girls St. Leo's High School and Aquinas Academy to become the first traditional Jesuit school to convert to coed, in the early 1970s. Bellarmine takes advantage of its setting with activities that reflect the outdoors and concern for the environment, including Earth Corps and Ski and Snowboarding Club.

Retreats are an important part of student life. About 95 percent of the student body annually participates in at least one. The St. Francis Xavier Plunge for freshmen culminates with students doing service with the homeless and the mentally and physically disabled. The Senior Pilgrimage is a two-day retreat in the Columbia Gorge that includes a ten-mile hike and Mass around a campfire.

Noted Alumni

Fr. Peter Henriot, SJ, director of the Jesuit Centre for Theological
    Reflection in Zambia
Leo Hindery, head of InterMedia Partners and business author
Rob Weller, entertainment entrepreneur and former host of
    Entertainment Tonight

— IHS —

Boston College High School

Location: Boston, Massachusetts
Founded: 1863
Number of Students: 1,300
Student Body: All-male
Nickname: Eagles

Interesting Information

BC High is located on a forty-acre campus on Boston Harbor and draws
students from eighty communities in eastern Massachusetts. It has more
than fifteen thousand living alumni. When BC High opened in 1863,
it enrolled twenty-two boys ranging in age from eleven to sixteen in a
first-year curriculum of Latin, Greek, theology, and philosophy. Today
Boston College High offers twenty-four advanced placement courses a
year, with 80 percent of students who take AP exams scoring a three or
higher. Under the school's academic enrichment program, one hundred
students travel overseas. The student-to-faculty ratio is 13:1.

The school also emphasizes community service. Its students assist
three hundred organizations in more than sixty communities. Each
year, seniors collectively perform about forty-five thousand hours of

service. The Mite Box, a student donation program, collects more than thirty thousand dollars a year for local charities. Other activities include a clothing drive for St. Francis House.

Noted Alumni

Harry Attridge, dean of Yale Divinity School

Ken Hackett, president and executive director of Catholic Relief Services

Dennis Lehane, author

John Murphy, chairman, president, and CEO of Oppenheimer Funds

Mike Sullivan, former NHL head coach

Michael White, chairman and CEO of PepsiCo International

Brebeuf Jesuit Preparatory School

Location: Indianapolis, Indiana
Founded: 1962
Number of Students: 800
Student Body: Coed
Nickname: Braves

Interesting Information

Brebeuf Jesuit Preparatory School calls itself "Jesuit, Catholic, and interfaith," serving a student body that is only about half Catholic. The school encourages students of all faiths to grow in their backgrounds and explore their values. Brebeuf is noted for its multicultural cocurricular activities and its ethnic-heritage organizations. The Lilly Endowment has awarded the school grants to promote a partnership with a private inner-city elementary school. Although Brebeuf has retained Braves as its nickname, it has removed all symbolic references to and images of Native Americans from the school.

Local news organizations have rated Brebeuf as Indianapolis's top school academically. Brebeuf emphasizes community service as part of its Ignatian identity.

Noted Alumni

Fr. Terry Charlton, SJ, founder of St. Aloysius Gonzaga High School in Nairobi
Alan Henderson, power forward for the Philadelphia 76ers
William Witchger, president of manufacturing company Marian Inc.

Brophy College Preparatory

Location: Phoenix, Arizona
Founded: 1928
Number of Students: 1,200
Student Body: All-male
Nickname: Broncos

Interesting Information

Brophy College Preparatory opened in 1928 on a seventeen-acre campus with three buildings, including Brophy Chapel, which features exquisite Spanish Colonial architecture and stained-glass windows created by Irish artists. The school's Manresa Retreat Center in Oak Creek Canyon offers a picturesque setting for prayer and reflection. Although Brophy was enthusiastically received when it opened, the timing was bad. After struggling during the Great Depression, it closed in 1935, reopening seventeen years later. It has added a number of buildings since, including a new library and one of Arizona's largest gymnasiums.

The Dottie Boreyko/Brophy Sports Campus is one of the nation's premier swim training facilities, consisting of two outdoor heated pools, one Olympic-sized with two underwater viewing rooms for stroke analysis and filming. The sports campus also includes a four-hundred-meter grass training track, a soccer field, locker rooms, and a full-size outdoor basketball court. A summer sports camp for elementary students features instruction in reading, math, writing, science, and arts and crafts as well as swimming.

Noted Alumni

Mark Alarie, former NBA forward
Gary Hall Jr. and John Simons, Olympic swimmers
Stephen Pyne, professor of life sciences at Arizona State University
Justin Speier, pitcher for the Los Angeles Angels

Canisius High School

Location: Buffalo, New York
Founded: 1870
Number of Students: 820
Student Body: All-male
Nickname: Crusaders

Interesting Information

To many people, Canisius High School has become known as "Tim Russert's alma mater," after the NBC Washington bureau chief's best-selling book *Big Russ & Me* painted an affectionate portrait of his years there. Canisius continues to attract many of the top students in western New York and southern Ontario, drawing from more than ninety elementary schools. It is proud that minority students compose about 20 percent of a typical freshman class.

Canisius has one of the nation's top crew programs, winning national titles in several categories in recent years. Service activities have included annual immersion trips to Camden, New Jersey, and a trip to Taos, New Mexico, to build a Habitat for Humanity home for a single parent.

Noted Alumni

Mark Russell, comedian, pianist, and singer
Tim Russert, senior vice president and Washington bureau chief of
  NBC News and host of *Meet the Press*

Cheverus High School

Location: Portland, Maine
Founded: 1917
Number of Students: 520
Student Body: Coed
Nickname: Stags

Interesting Information

Cheverus High School opened as a diocesan school in 1917 and became a Jesuit school in 1942. The twenty-five-acre campus in a scenic residential area boasts an outdoor sporting complex that includes a football/

soccer/lacrosse/track facility built within a natural amphitheater. The school has created a corporate sponsorship and advertising program for athletics that generates funds for scholarships and the school's operations.

Cheverus's varied program of cocurriculars takes advantage of its location. Its Outdoor Club offers rock-climbing classes at the Maine Rock Gym and takes members snowshoeing and hiking in Acadia National Park and other Maine islands.

Noted Alumni

Joseph Brennan, former governor of Maine
Ian Crocker, Olympic swimmer
John, James, and Leon Gorman, owners of L. L. Bean

~ IHS ~

Colegio San Ignacio de Loyola

Location: Rio Piedras, San Juan, Puerto Rico
Founded: 1952
Number of Students: 722
Student Body: All-male

Interesting Information

Colegio San Ignacio de Loyola is considered one of Puerto Rico's most prestigious secondary schools. The school has enjoyed strong leadership from individuals such as Fr. Francisco Jose "Pepito" Marrero, SJ, the longtime school chaplain. Despite suffering from Parkinson's disease, he runs the Jajome Program, which provides spiritual therapy for faculty, students, parents, and married persons. A former student said that Marrero's "hands may shiver, and sometimes it is difficult to understand him when he speaks, but you can sense his spiritual firmness, and he is able to look up to God despite the obstacles that he encounters in his path."

Another significant figure is Maria del Carmen Garay, social worker and coordinator of the Guidance Department. She has helped economically deprived students attend Colegio San Ignacio by organizing the Programa Proyecto, which provides scholarships. If she finds a student with potential who cannot get a scholarship to Colegio San Ignacio, she helps him enter another school. A doctor who graduated from San Ignacio cited the "extreme importance" of her influence in his life and said she deserves his "eternal gratitude."

Noted Alumni

Antonio Dajer, acting director of the New York Downtown Hospital Emergency Department

Raul Julia, actor and Hunger Project advocate

Fr. Fernando Pico, SJ, priest and writer

― IHS ―

Creighton Preparatory School

Location: Omaha, Nebraska
Founded: 1878
Number of Students: 1,025
Student Body: All-male
Nickname: Junior Bluejays

Interesting Information

Creighton Prep was originally part of Creighton University. Both were named in honor of Edward Creighton, who amassed a fortune building the nation's first transcontinental telegraph line; a bequest from the Creighton family endowed the schools.

Creighton Prep is noted for creating the Prep freshman retreat, which about a dozen other Jesuit high schools have adopted, and for its collaboration with local Catholic schools in Operation Others, which feeds about fifteen hundred families at Christmas. Prep's Academic Decathlon teams have been among the best of their size, finishing second nationally twice between 2004 and 2006. During that same period, Prep twice received the *Omaha World-Herald*'s All-Sports Trophy (Boys Division) for Class A schools for its overall athletic excellence.

Noted Alumni

Fr. Bob Dufford, SJ, and Fr. Robert "Roc" O'Connor, SJ, members of
    the St. Louis Jesuits musical group
Ron Hansen, novelist and professor of English at Santa Clara
    University
Alexander Payne, director
Michael Ryan, former chief of staff of the U.S. Air Force
Charles, Frank, Joseph, and Martin Vacanti, medical researchers

— IHS —

Cristo Rey High School

Location: Sacramento, California
Founded: 2006

Number of Students: 105 (freshmen only)
Student Body: Coed

Interesting Information

Cristo Rey High School opened in the fall of 2006 as the newest member of the Cristo Rey Network. It offers a quality Catholic college preparatory education to low-income students who finance their education through a Corporate Internship Program.

— IHS —

Cristo Rey Jesuit High School

Location: Chicago, Illinois
Founded: 1996
Number of Students: 525
Student Body: Coed
Nickname: Cristeros

Interesting Information

Cristo Rey serves one of the most densely populated and least formally educated neighborhoods in Chicago. It created a work-study model to keep Catholic schools serving low-income students alive in inner-city neighborhoods, and the Cristo Rey Network assists other cities in creating similar schools. Cristo Rey's success has drawn national attention, including features on *60 Minutes* and articles in the *New York Times* and the *Washington Post*, among others.

Cristo Rey offers a dual-language program in Spanish and English to promote proficiency. In spite of the demands of the work-study program, students participate in a variety of sports, campus ministry, and other cocurricular activities.

— IHS —

De Smet Jesuit High School

Location: Creve Coeur, Missouri
Founded: 1967
Number of Students: 1,250
Student Body: All-male
Nickname: Spartans

Interesting Information

De Smet Jesuit High School students live the school motto "Men for others" by annually raising more than fifty thousand dollars to support Jesuit missions in Central America and other charitable organizations. They also do more than forty-five thousand hours of service work in the community each year and collect more than nine thousand cans of food to donate to local agencies.

De Smet encourages every student to be involved in extracurricular activities. Over eight hundred students participate in at least one sport, many in two or three. The school has forty-six teams in eighteen sports and more than thirty clubs and organizations. De Smet's partnerships with Hewlett-Packard and Microsoft give students and faculty access to state-of-the-art technology.

Noted Alumni

Henry Autrey, district judge of the Eastern District of Missouri
Frank J. Cusumano, sportscaster

Joseph Duggan, senior policy adviser for the U.S. Agency for
International Development

Bill Mueller, third baseman for the Los Angeles Dodgers

~ IHS ~

Fairfield College Preparatory School

Location: Fairfield, Connecticut
Founded: 1942
Number of Students: 900
Student Body: All-male
Nickname: Jesuits

Interesting Information

Fairfield College Preparatory School shares a two-hundred-acre semi-
rural campus overlooking Long Island Sound with Fairfield University.
Its first classroom building was the original Jennings mansion, while
the former Lashar mansion became the Jesuit residence. The original
graduating class, in 1943, had eleven students.

Fairfield Prep's location gives students access to the university's
facilities, including the 275,000-volume DiMenna-Nyselius Library;
the Recreation Complex, with an indoor swimming pool and basketball, racquetball, and tennis courts; the Quick Center for the Arts; and
the Egan Chapel of St. Ignatius Loyola. Students come to Fairfield
Prep from fifty-one towns across Connecticut. About 10 percent are
students of color.

Noted Alumni

Chris Drury, center for the Buffalo Sabres

Sean McManus, president of CBS News and CBS Sports
Bob Skoronski, former NFL offensive captain

~ IHS ~

Fordham Preparatory School

Location: Bronx, New York
Founded: 1841
Number of Students: 915
Student Body: All-male
Nickname: Rams

Interesting Information

Fordham Prep, located on the campus of Fordham University, in the Bronx, is the nation's fifth-oldest Jesuit high school and has over ten thousand alums living in forty-eight states and forty countries. It is noted for its classical curriculum.

Fordham Prep has produced numerous noted alums, including such members of the Baseball Hall of Fame as Frankie Frisch, "the Fordham Flash," who managed the St. Louis Cardinals in the 1930s (when they were known as the Gashouse Gang); and Vin Scully, the longtime voice of the Dodgers, who also is in the Radio Hall of Fame. Another legendary alum is Arthur Daley, former sports columnist for the *New York Times*, who won a Pulitzer Prize.

Fordham Prep still produces strong students, athletes, and "men for others" such as Dr. Bill Magee, a medical missionary who started Operation Smile, which provides reconstructive surgery for poor children worldwide. A student organization at Fordham Prep, Operation Smile and Beyond, supports his work.

Noted Alumni

Arthur Daley, former sports columnist

Frankie Frisch, former MLB player and manager

Bill Magee, cofounder of Operation Smile

Cardinal Theodore McCarrick, archbishop emeritus of Washington, DC

Vin Scully, radio announcer for the Los Angeles Dodgers

~ IHS ~

Georgetown Preparatory School

Location: Bethesda, Maryland

Founded: 1789

Number of Students: 435

Student Body: All-male

Nickname: Little Hoyas

Interesting Information

Georgetown Preparatory School is the nation's oldest Jesuit school and the only Jesuit boarding school. About one hundred of its students are boarders. Its founder, John Carroll, SJ, was the first bishop of the United States. Its students have included members of George Washington's family and, in another era, members of the Kennedy family, such as Anthony Shriver, cofounder of Best Buddies, an international organization that fosters friendships between people with intellectual disabilities and people who are not disabled.

Georgetown Prep students come from nineteen states and twenty-three foreign countries. In keeping with its international emphasis, the school offers a full English-as-a-Second-Language program, through which students supplement their study of English with other courses. They gradually integrate into the regular curriculum as English proficiency increases.

Noted Alumni

William Bidwell, owner of the Arizona Cardinals
Brian Cashman, general manager of the New York Yankees
John Dingell, U.S. representative for Michigan
Christopher Dodd, U.S. senator for Connecticut
Christopher Rogers, cofounder of Nextel Communications
L. Francis Rooney, U.S. ambassador to the Vatican

— IHS —

Gonzaga College High School

Location: Washington, DC
Founded: 1821
Number of Students: 900
Student Body: All-male
Nickname: Eagles

Interesting Information

Gonzaga College High School holds a federal charter signed by President James Buchanan in 1858 that allows it to grant college degrees, although the higher education program at Gonzaga died out many years ago. The school is adjacent to historic and recently renovated St. Aloysius Church, which was completed just before the Civil War. To escape being converted to a Union hospital like other churches,

St. Aloysius Parish built a wartime hospital on its grounds. John Philip Sousa at one time directed the school's band.

Gonzaga, a ten-minute walk from Union Station, was within a mile of the riots that broke out following the assassination of Martin Luther King Jr. It lost nearly half its enrollment and was threatened with either closing or relocating, but alums and the Maryland Province of the Jesuits were committed to keeping the school in its location. In recent years, the *Wall Street Journal* has called it the premier Catholic high school in Washington.

Noted Alumni

William Bennett, former U. S. secretary of education
Pat Buchanan, former senior adviser to the White House
Joseph Ellis, historian
Martin O'Malley, governor of Maryland
John Thompson III, head basketball coach at Georgetown University

— IHS —

Gonzaga Preparatory High School

Location: Spokane, Washington
Founded: 1887
Number of Students: 870
Student Body: Coed
Nickname: Bullpups

Interesting Information

Gonzaga Prep, located on a twenty-acre campus in north Spokane, offers a mission-driven tuition plan, whereby families pay according to guidelines based on adjusted gross income. This is a school committed to service. Each year, students donate more than 11,500 hours of service and conduct a Thanksgiving food drive that collects more than one hundred thousand pounds of food and feeds four hundred families. The school offers annual retreats for all students, faculty, and staff. About 85 percent of the students participate in one or more school-organized activities.

Gonzaga works to keep the school affordable through an annual fund drive and an auction and encouragement of planned giving. It has managed to keep annual increases in cost per student below five percent from 2002 to 2006.

Noted Alumni

Bing Crosby, singer and actor
Tom Foley, former speaker of the House of Representatives

— IHS —

Jesuit College Preparatory School of Dallas

Location: Dallas, Texas
Founded: 1942
Number of Students: 1,020
Student Body: All-male
Nickname: Rangers

Interesting Information

In 1965, Dallas Jesuit became the first integrated high school in Texas, one of its proudest claims to fame. It is also home to a museum that features the works of international artists such as Francisco Zúñiga,

Dale Chihuly, Christo, and Dalí. Numerous grade school and middle school groups tour the museum, getting an introduction to Dallas Jesuit in the process. Special exhibits draw media attention. Visiting artists are requested to design a T-shirt and donate a portion of its sales to the museum.

Jesuit stresses service. Students are required to donate 150 hours of service to the Dallas community. Following Hurricane Katrina, in the fall of 2005, the school accepted seventy New Orleans Jesuit transfer students and integrated them into its classes until they could return home.

Noted Alumni

Ryan Cabrera, musician
Kenny Cooper, forward for FC Dallas
Bill DeOre, political cartoonist for the *Dallas Morning News*
Pat Schnitzius, proprietor of Bartush-Schnitzius Foods

Jesuit High School (New Orleans)

Location: New Orleans, Louisiana
Founded: 1847
Number of Students: 1,425
Student Body: All-male
Nickname: Blue Jays

Interesting Information

When Hurricane Katrina devastated New Orleans in 2005, almost six feet of water inundated Jesuit High School's entire first floor and physical education facility for more than two weeks. Nevertheless, Jesuit was the first flooded school in New Orleans to reopen, after Thanksgiving 2005. The school sought donations for the five million dollars in expenses not covered by insurance, and extensive repairs continued for months. These included reconstruction of the auditorium, installation of new elevators, electrical repairs, and extensive work on the kitchen. Other Jesuit schools and students raised funds to help Jesuit with this catastrophe.

Nearly all of Jesuit's khaki-clad students returned in the spring semester of 2006. While displaced, many had attended other Jesuit high schools, including Houston's Strake Jesuit College Preparatory, where about four hundred boys had enrolled in a "school within a school" created by Strake and New Orleans Jesuit faculty. School officials say New Orleans Jesuit will continue to anchor its Mid-City neighborhood.

Noted Alumni

Will Clark, former MLB first baseman
Harry Connick Jr., singer, musician, and actor
Marc Morial, former mayor of New Orleans
Jay Thomas, actor and radio personality
Don Wetzel, inventor of the ATM

— IHS —

Jesuit High School (Portland)

Location: Portland, Oregon
Founded: 1956
Number of Students: 1,150

Student Body: Coed
Nickname: Crusaders

Interesting Information

A Portland Jesuit student who runs into a snag with homework or research can get help with the click of a mouse. Jesuit's Web site provides a link to L-Net, an Oregon library program that allows students to contact a librarian for help around the clock. This is just one way that the school integrates technology into instruction. When history teacher Jerry Hahn moved to Germany to teach English as a foreign language on a Fulbright Teacher Exchange, he started a blog on the school's Web site so that Portland Jesuit students could follow his experiences.

Jesuit emphasizes both service and reflection on that service. One recent year, seniors gave 31,847 hours of service. Here are a few samples of their reflections: "The homeless don't have nearly as much as I do; however, that leaves room for their faith to become extremely strong." "God bless the children [at St. Andrew's Nativity School] who begin to teach, and God bless the teachers who begin to love like the children." "I haven't really thought about my work spiritually, but now I believe more in people and in myself. Like Dorothy Day said, it's a circle of giving and receiving. I thought if I was going to make a difference I had to go big, but doing this service work I now know that touching someone's life and being touched by them is the biggest contribution to the world I can make."

Noted Alumni

Tim Boyle, president and CEO of Columbia Sportswear
Pete Brock, former NFL lineman
Stan Brock, head coach of the Army football team and former NFL lineman

Mandy Bruno, actress
Ed Cody, foreign correspondent for the *Washington Post*
Kate Johnson, Olympic rower
John Merriman, professor of history at Yale University
Erik Spoelstra, assistant coach of the Miami Heat

— IHS —

Jesuit High School (Sacramento)

Location: Sacramento, California
Founded: 1963
Number of Students: 1,000
Student Body: All-male
Nickname: Marauders

Interesting Information

Sacramento's Jesuit High School is the nation's rugby powerhouse. In 2006, the Marauders won the USA Rugby Tier A Championship. The *Sacramento Bee* carries numerous articles about Jesuit's prowess in the sport and noted that the University of California at Berkeley won the collegiate rugby title with the assistance of Jesuit alum Louis Stanfill, the tournament's MVP. Jesuit was opened in 1963, during the height of the Space Race, and considered adopting the nickname Space Cadets.

Jesuit expects two things from its students: that they go to college and help the community. Students who participate in the Loaves and Fishes Overnight Immersion Plunge arrive incognito at the downtown food-distribution program for the homeless. They stay overnight and eat soup kitchen fare—miles away from their comfort zones.

Noted Alumni

Ken O'Brien, former NFL quarterback
Vince Brooks, former public affairs director for the army
Mark Glassy, immunologist, entrepreneur, and science fiction
 collector

— IHS —

Jesuit High School of Tampa

Location: Tampa, Florida
Founded: 1899
Number of Students: 650
Student Body: All-male
Nickname: Tigers

Interesting Information

Jesuit is noted for the extraordinary loyalty and generosity of its alumni. In 1968, the school won its first state football championship. Thirty-five years later, every member of that team contributed to fully fund an endowment for the school. "We were the beneficiaries of people with vision, love, persistence, generosity, and hope. It's our time to give something back to a place that gave us so much," wrote one former player.

Both a classroom and a golf classic honor the memory of Fr. Richard G. Hartnett, SJ, who graduated from Jesuit in 1930 and spent almost forty years teaching English, Latin, and religion. He was noted for his kindness, especially to a severely disabled former student to whom he took communion and whom he encouraged students to assist. Service programs abound at Tampa Jesuit. The Dads' Club runs a Buccaneers

Parking program at Tampa Bay Buccaneers home games that raised more than one hundred thousand dollars for Jesuit in 2005.

The school has produced numerous well-known athletes, including late former White Sox manager Al Lopez Sr., class of '27, who was the oldest living member of the Baseball Hall of Fame before he died in 2005. Tampa Jesuit named its athletic center after him.

Noted Alumni

Ron Busuttil, chief of the division of liver and pancreas transplant at
    UCLA
Michael Doyle, former assistant secretary general of the United
    Nations
Anthony Lazzara Jr., founder of Villa la Paz clinic in Peru
Al Lopez Sr., former MLB catcher and manager
Lou Piniella, manager of the Chicago Cubs

Loyola Academy

Location: Wilmette, Illinois
Founded: 1909
Number of Students: 2,000
Student Body: Coed
Nickname: Ramblers

Interesting Information

Loyola Academy is the nation's largest Jesuit high school, serving suburban Chicago. Its facilities include the sixty-acre Glenview campus, a combination of athletic complex and nature center. Not only can students play various sports on the campus's outstanding fields, but they can also visit a nature preserve that contains part of the north branch of the Chicago River. This habitat for endangered wildlife is a living laboratory for students in environmental science, biology, and chemistry classes. Loyola Academy offers 110 different courses, one of the nation's most comprehensive high school curricula.

Students from eighty different ZIP codes in the Chicago area attend Loyola. In addition to academics, they can participate in a wide range of sports, such as sailing on Lake Michigan and water polo in an indoor pool. Summer service opportunities include immersion trips to sites in the United States, Mexico, and Peru.

Noted Alumni

Bill Murray, actor and comedian
Peter F. Steinfels, religion reporter for the *New York Times*
Chris O'Donnell, actor
Bill Plante, reporter for CBS News

Loyola Blakefield

Location: Towson, Maryland
Founded: 1852
Number of Students: 1,000 (grades 6–12)
Student Body: All-male
Nickname: Dons

Interesting Information

Loyola Blakefield has served the Baltimore area since 1852, moving to its current location north of the city in 1934–41. Students come from the city, six surrounding counties, and the southern counties of Pennsylvania. Between 1981 and 1988, the school gradually introduced middle school classes and changed its name from Loyola High School to Loyola Blakefield in recognition of the two levels of education.

Loyola Blakefield's campus ministry program offers a variety of retreats, including prayer groups for mothers and fathers based on the Spiritual Exercises, the Sophomore Father-Son Retreat, and the Junior Mother-Son Retreat. The campus ministry office arranges individual annual Christian service projects as well as class and homeroom projects, such as working with mentally and physically disabled children and teens and helping at soup kitchens. These class experiences begin in sixth grade. Middle school students also participate in retreats.

Noted Alumni

Tom Clancy, author
Nathaniel Fick, author and former U.S. Marine Corps officer
Jim McKay, sportscaster

— IHS —

Loyola High School

Location: Detroit, Michigan
Founded: 1993
Number of Students: 160

Student Body: All-male
Nickname: Bulldogs

Interesting Information

Loyola's mission is to nurture "a culture of hope and academic success for young men in Detroit challenged by an urban environment." This small school was founded after the Detroit Board of Education proposed starting all-male academies to reduce the alarming dropout rate of high school boys. When the court ruled that it was unconstitutional for public schools to be single sex, the Jesuits opened such a school. Loyola makes it a priority to serve young men who are in danger of dropping out and are not working up to their academic and social potential. The school stresses academic basics. It invites speakers to discuss topics such as what happens to teens involved in gangs, drugs, and violent crimes.

To defray their tuition, all juniors and seniors work one day a week plus one Friday a month at an entry-level clerical position. Students gain work experience and apply what they have learned in the classroom in a real-world setting.

― IHS ―

Loyola High School of Los Angeles Jesuit Prep

Location: Los Angeles, California
Founded: 1865
Number of Students: 1,215
Student Body: All-male
Nickname: Cubs

Interesting Information

Loyola High School of Los Angeles is the oldest secondary school in southern California, run by the Jesuits since 1911. Originally, it was part of St. Vincent's College, ancestor of Loyola Marymount University. Loyola High School occupies the original twenty-acre campus in central Los Angeles. The newest addition to this campus is a science and technology building, constructed in 2005.

Loyola's programs include an annual Senior Project, a three-week immersion program in which each Loyola senior contributes a minimum of eighty-five hours of service. Seniors research, propose, and negotiate a daytime service project with groups such as inner-city schools (both Catholic and public), special-education programs, homeless shelters, homes for the aged, and community service centers. The Los Angeles City Council and others have honored the project.

Noted Alumni

Fr. Gordon Bennett, SJ, former bishop of Mandeville, Jamaica

Fr. Greg Boyle, SJ, minister to gang members

John Debney, film composer

Leo Lagasse, surgeon and professor emeritus of obstetrics and gynecology at UCLA

Edward P. Roski, chairman and CEO of Majestic Realty and part owner of the L.A. Lakers and the L.A. Kings

Matt Ware, defensive back for the Arizona Cardinals

Anthony A. Williams, former mayor of Washington, DC

— IHS —

Loyola School

Location: New York, New York
Founded: 1900
Number of Students: 200
Student Body: Coed
Nickname: Knights

Interesting Information

Loyola School was founded as a boys school but went coed in 1973, the only coed Jesuit school in its region. The school, which draws students from all five boroughs, New Jersey, and Westchester County, is located two blocks east of Central Park and Museum Mile in the residential area on the Upper East Side of Manhattan. With a student-teacher ratio of 9:1 and an average class size of fifteen, it encourages personal attention and individual participation.

Loyola integrates Christian service into its educational program. It has received the Above and Beyond Award from WABC-TV for having a positive impact on the community through its Wellington T. Mara Christian Service Program and the Brownbaggers Club.

Noted Alumnus

Wellington Mara, former owner of the New York Giants

— IHS —

Marquette University High School

Location: Milwaukee, Wisconsin
Founded: 1857
Number of Students: 1,075

Student Body: All-male
Nickname: Hilltoppers

Interesting Information

Marquette University High School is located in the historic Merrill Park neighborhood. The school sponsors a program with the Merrill Park Neighborhood Association in which students volunteer to help the neighborhood in areas of education, housing, and recreation/outreach. Sophomores are required to perform twenty-four hours of service, juniors sixty-five hours, and seniors eighty hours, through the Senior Shared Life Program.

The school is noted for its success in national forensics and debate competition and also enjoys national success in math and science competition. Its minority student enrollment is 22 percent.

Noted Alumni

Tom Barrett, mayor of Milwaukee
Fr. Don Doll, SJ, photographer and professor at Creighton University
Tom Fox, former publisher of the *National Catholic Reporter*
E. Michael McCann, former district attorney for Milwaukee
Tom Snyder, TV talk show host
John Stollenwerk, president and CEO of Allen-Edmonds Shoe
    Corporation

— IHS —

McQuaid Jesuit High School

Location: Rochester, New York
Founded: 1954

Number of Students: 880 (grades 7–12)
Student Body: All-male
Nickname: Knights

Interesting Information

McQuaid Jesuit has shown its diversity through its Xavier Scholars program, which provides five scholarships to students from six inner-city Catholic elementary schools. Because McQuaid also has a middle school, the scholarships are for six years, giving these students two years to prepare for the rigors of a Jesuit high school education along with their new classmates.

Like all Jesuit schools, McQuaid stresses a combination of scholarship, athletics, and service. Its teams have won numerous sectional championships in addition to a number of regional and state championships in sports such as basketball and hockey. Through the school's Christian service program, MAGIS, upperclassmen are released from school to work with the elderly, the infirm, and the disabled. Service carries over into adult life. For example, alum Jerry Jones climbed Mount Kilimanjaro in honor of a classmate who was battling ALS.

Noted Alumni

Jim Clapp, professor emeritus of urban planning at San Diego State
    University
A. Neil Pappalardo, founder, chairman, and CEO of Meditech
David Schickler, novelist
Robert Thomas, chief justice of the Illinois Supreme Court
Dan Warmenhoven, CEO of Network Appliance

— IHS —

Red Cloud High School

Location: Pine Ridge, South Dakota
Founded: 1888
Number of Students: 215
Student Body: Coed
Nickname: Crusaders

Interesting Information

This school on the Pine Ridge Reservation was founded as a boarding school run by the Holy Rosary Mission and serving boys and girls from elementary grades through high school. It celebrates its students' Lakota heritage with a Lakota studies program and a theology program that emphasizes both Catholic and Lakota spirituality. The school begins its graduation ceremony with a graduation powwow and a feather ceremony.

The thirty-five-member class of 2006 included six winners of highly competitive Gates Millennium Scholarships, which pay all college expenses. Red Cloud High School is one of eleven schools participating in NASA's THEMIS Project. In 2006, a Red Cloud student won first place in the National Science Fair for the third year in a row.

Noted Alumni

Laurel Iron Cloud, associate judge of the Fort McDowell Yavapai tribe
Patrick Lee, former chief judge of the Oglala Sioux tribe
Delphine Red Shirt, professor and author
Charles E. Trimble, journalist, author, and Native American cultural activist
Dena Wilson, physician

— IHS —

Regis High School

Location: New York, New York
Founded: 1914
Number of Students: 530
Student Body: All-male
Nickname: Raiders

Interesting Information

Since its founding in 1914, Regis High School has offered free tuition to all of its students. A generous parishioner of the Church of St. Ignatius Loyola wanted to make Jesuit education accessible to bright but poor boys, so she and her family supported the school until the 1960s, when Regis alums joined the family in the effort. Strong alumni support has allowed Regis to remain tuition-free. Alums maintain their ties to Regis through specialized alumni groups such as the Regis Bar Association and the Regis Business Network.

In 2002, Regis started the REACH program to prepare middle school students from inner-city Catholic schools to be competitive for its entrance exam and the scholarship exams of other Jesuit and Catholic high schools. Regis students come from all parts of New York City and suburban areas in New York, Connecticut, and New Jersey. Regis has a student-teacher ratio of 10:1.

Noted Alumni

Edward Conlon, author and police officer
Anthony Fauci, director of the National Institute of Allergy and
    Infectious Diseases
Patrick Fitzgerald, U.S. attorney for the Northern District of Illinois

Fr. Timothy Healy, SJ, late former president of Georgetown
University and former head of the New York Public Library

— IHS —

Regis Jesuit High School

Location: Aurora, Colorado
Founded: 1877
Number of Students: 1,350
Student Body: Co-institutional
Nickname: Raiders

Interesting Information

Regis Jesuit High School, located in a Denver suburb, is the nation's only
co-institutional Jesuit high school. It offers single-gender education for
both young men and young women by operating two separate divisions
in separate buildings. Each has its own principal, administrative team,
faculty, and staff. The school provides students with what it calls the best
of both worlds—"a structured academic environment during the school
day with coed social opportunities after school and at school events."

Regis's strong academic program allows qualified students to
earn up to thirty-six hours of college credit from Regis University—
the only high school in the Denver metropolitan area with such an
arrangement.

Noted Alumni

A. Benedict Cosimi, chief of transplantation at Massachusetts
General Hospital and past president of the American Society of
Transplant Surgeons

John Carroll Lynch, actor
Dan McVicar, actor
Fr. Carl Reinert, SJ, late former president of Creighton University

— IHS —

Rockhurst High School

Location: Kansas City, Missouri
Founded: 1910
Number of Students: 1,040
Student Body: All-male
Nickname: Hawklets

Interesting Information

Rockhurst High School draws its name from its original setting on a stony piece of ground near a wooded area. Originally, it was called the Academy of Rockhurst College, changing its name in 1923. Today it is located near the Missouri-Kansas state line and serves students from throughout the greater Kansas City area.

Rockhurst High is noted for its outstanding journalism program. In 2005–06, the *Prep News* won first place with special merit from the American Scholastic Press Association (ASPA), the highest critical award. It was also one of seven newspapers nationally to receive ASPA's Most Outstanding High School Newspaper for 2005–06. Judges commended the "superior academic coverage of your newspaper" and urged that it be "shared with neighboring schools in your area." Rockhurst also emphasizes service, requiring students to give twenty-five hours a year during their first three years, especially in direct service to the poor.

Noted Alumni

Robert Callahan, former president of ABC
David Cone, former MLB pitcher
Tim Kaine, governor of Virginia
Joseph Teasdale, former governor of Missouri

— IHS —

St. Ignatius College Prep (Chicago)

Location: Chicago, Illinois
Founded: 1869
Number of Students: 1,350
Student Body: Coed
Nickname: The Wolfpack

Interesting Information

St. Ignatius College Prep is located in a magnificent five-building campus that includes one of the few buildings to survive the Chicago fire of 1871. This original building, a national historic landmark, first housed St. Ignatius College, today's Loyola University. One of the school's buildings also was the first site of Chicago's Field Museum of Natural History and still displays some specimens. The National Trust for Historic Preservation has honored St. Ignatius College Prep for its restoration efforts. Its campus features a view of the city skyline.

However, St. Ignatius is more than carved oak paneling, wrought iron railings, exquisite millwork, and stained glass. It draws students from throughout the metro area and as far away as southern Wisconsin by offering them two Internet-connected libraries with more than thirty thousand volumes, state-of-the-art science and language labs, a theater, two full-sized gymnasiums, a wrestling and fitness center, tennis courts, and athletic fields. It also has one of the nation's top classics programs.

Noted Alumni

William Daley, former U.S. secretary of commerce
Mellody Hobson, president of Aerial Capital Management
Fr. Daniel Lord, SJ, writer
Bob Newhart, comedian and actor

— IHS —

St. Ignatius College Preparatory (San Francisco)

Location: San Francisco, California
Founded: 1855
Number of Students: 1,415
Student Body: Coed
Nickname: Wildcats

Interesting Information

The first Jesuits arrived in San Francisco in 1849 along with the gold rush and six years later opened "SI Prep," the city's oldest private high school. Originally, it was part of the University of San Francisco. The school lost its building in the 1906 earthquake and fire but rebuilt on a temporary campus that lasted twenty-three years. Today's beautiful campus in the Sunset District is its sixth. The school offers topflight science facilities. An alum, John Montgomery (class of 1878), was an aviation pioneer and the first person to fly a glider, near San Diego in 1883.

St. Ignatius College Preparatory is noted for the strength of its Ignatian identity and its work in faculty spirituality. Its adult spirituality office helps faculty and staff integrate Ignatian ideals into their lives.

Noted Alumni

Jerry Brown, attorney general for California
Dan Fouts, former NFL quarterback
Eric Goosby, CEO of Pangaea Global AIDS Foundation
Peter Raven, director of the Missouri Botanical Garden
Fr. Carlos Sevilla, SJ, bishop of Yakima, Washington

— IHS —

St. Ignatius High School

Location: Cleveland, Ohio
Founded: 1886
Number of Students: 1,430
Student Body: All-male
Nickname: Wildcats

Interesting Information

The German Jesuits who founded St. Ignatius High School modeled it after the German Gymnasium and the French lycée, European secondary schools. They admitted students after six years of grammar school, then awarded them a bachelor's degree after six more years. There was no division between the high school and the college programs until 1902. In 1923, the college changed its name to John Carroll University and moved locations, leaving the original campus to St. Ignatius High.

Today's campus includes thirteen buildings on sixteen acres. Its North German Gothic building, designed by a Dutch Jesuit architect, is designated as Cleveland Landmark No. 59.

In 2006, NPR joined local media in publicizing the school's St. Joseph of Arimathea Society, which trains students to serve as pallbearers for those who die without relatives and friends. This is just part of a strong campus ministry program that works with the poor and homeless. The school also offers a *cura personalis* intervention program to support academic achievement for students experiencing health and emotional problems.

Noted Alumni

Charles Dolan, founder and chairman of Cablevision
Larry Dolan, owner of the Cleveland Indians
Charles Geschke, cofounder of Adobe Systems
Tim Mack, Olympic pole vaulter
Kenneth L. Woodward, religion writer

St. John's Jesuit High School

Location: Toledo, Ohio
Founded: 1965
Number of Students: 850
Student Body: All-male
Nickname: Titans

Interesting Information

Although the founding date of St. John's Jesuit is listed as 1965, it was once part of St. John's University, which was founded in 1898 by

German Jesuits who had been expelled from their homeland as part of Bismarck's Kulturkampf. Until World War I, St. John's students were required to study German. The high school was forced to close during the Great Depression, but alumni kept their Jesuit heritage and traditions alive through reunions and a play dealing with Jesuit life, *The First Legion*, whose ticket sales benefited Jesuit education. In the 1960s, the Jesuits reopened St. John's on an estate near Toledo. It was the first school in northwest Ohio to have central heat and air-conditioning.

Today St. John's Jesuit provides over $1.5 million in tuition assistance and offers a minority scholarship program, called the Toledo 2020 Scholars Program, and career exploration classes in law and engineering. Its athletes have won the City League All-Sports trophy for twenty-five out of thirty-three years. St. John's also leads its area in National Merit finalists. The school stresses Ignatian spirituality with opportunities for student and adult retreats, prayer groups, and liturgies.

Noted Alumni

John Amaechi, former NBA center
Nick Anderson, editorial cartoonist
Doug Ducey, chairman and CEO of Cold Stone Creamery
Steve Hartman, correspondent for CBS News
Scott Parsons, member of 2004 Olympic whitewater slalom team
Mike Sallah, reporter

— IHS —

St. Joseph's Preparatory School

Location: Philadelphia, Pennsylvania
Founded: 1851

Number of Students: 930
Student Body: All-male
Nickname: Hawks

Interesting Information

St. Joseph's Preparatory School traces its origins to a small church that a Jesuit founded in central Philadelphia in 1733. Originally, the school was part of St. Joseph's College, but the two separated, and the college left all its buildings on the current West Girard Avenue site to the high school. Early high school students attended classes from 8:00 a.m. to 5:00 p.m., with a long lunch break to permit them to go home. They maintained silence in chapel, classrooms, and hallways. They were to leave for home immediately after school and had prescribed morning and evening study hours at home. In 1966, a fire destroyed two-thirds of the school, but it rebuilt in its traditional urban environment despite pressure to move to the suburbs.

Today's St. Joseph's stresses service to its North Philadelphia neighborhood. Its Ignatian service office helps place juniors and seniors in projects that will meet their service requirements. Students come to St. Joseph's from throughout Philadelphia, surrounding Pennsylvania counties, and southern New Jersey.

Noted Alumni

Fr. John Foley, archbishop and former president of the Pontifical
   Council for Social Communications
Matt Guokas Jr., former NBA head coach
Alexander Haig Jr., former U.S. secretary of state
Phil Martelli, head basketball coach at St. Joseph's University
Andrew von Eschenbach, commissioner of the Food and Drug
   Administration

~ IHS ~

St. Louis University High School

Location: St. Louis, Missouri
Founded: 1818
Number of Students: 1,065
Student Body: All-male
Nickname: Jr. Billikens

Interesting Information

St. Louis University High School is the nation's second-oldest Jesuit high school and the oldest private Catholic high school west of the Mississippi. It began as a Latin school called St. Louis Academy. The early school took in boarders and charged them $120 annually for "fuel and servants." In 1888–89, it separated from St. Louis University.

Throughout its history, SLU High School has constantly upgraded its curriculum and facilities. Today's average class size is twenty, down from thirty a number of years ago, thanks to a larger faculty and fourteen new classrooms. It also improved its athletic facilities.

SLU High School offers more than eighty-five elective courses and advanced placement classes in nineteen disciplines. It maintains community partnerships with notable local institutions such as the St. Louis Science Center, Barnes-Jewish Hospital, and Forest Park Forever. SLU High School is ranked in the top 7 percent of schools nationally for its composite ACT score. All seniors perform 120 hours of service during January.

Noted Alumni

Tom Dooley, physician, humanitarian, and recipient of the
   Congressional Gold Medal

E. Michael Harrington, author and professor of music business at
    Belmont University
Robert Hyland, former general manager of KMOX and creator of the
    talk radio format
Henry Jones, former NFL defensive back
Ed Macauley, deacon and former NBA center

~ IHS ~

St. Peter's Prep

Location: Jersey City, New Jersey
Founded: 1872
Number of Students: 940
Student Body: All-male
Nickname: Marauders

Interesting Information

St. Peter's Prep boasts a majestic view of the nearby Statue of Liberty,
with the New York skyline to the east. It sits in the historic Paulus
Hook neighborhood, filled with century-old brownstones. Six buildings make up today's high school. Shalloe Hall, the original structure,
was built to house both St. Peter's College and the high school.

St. Peter's Prep foreign language students can expand their cultural horizons through student exchange programs with Catholic high
schools in France, Germany, and Italy, in addition to participating in
faculty-led summer trips to France, Spain, and Mexico. Spirituality programs include mother-son and father-son retreats, service to the homeless in Hoboken, and fund-raising for Jesuit mission work worldwide.

Noted Alumni

Philip Bosco, actor
Will Durant, historian
Thomas Fleming, historian and author
Nathan Lane, actor

~ IHS ~

St. Xavier High School

Location: Cincinnati, Ohio
Founded: 1831
Number of Students: 1,500
Student Body: All-male
Nickname: Bombers

Interesting Information

St. Xavier is the largest all-male Jesuit high school in the United States and was founded in connection with Xavier University. It sits on a 110-acre campus and draws students from northern Kentucky and southeastern Indiana as well as Cincinnati. Under St. Xavier's house system, freshmen are grouped into five "houses," sharing an English teacher, a religion teacher, and a world cultures teacher with their housemates. Students name their houses, usually after Jesuit saints, and form social and spiritual bonds through field trips, retreats, and other activities.

Three-fourths of the students voluntarily participate in community service. Popular programs include Big Buddies, in which boys become mentors for members of the Boys and Girls Clubs of Greater Cincinnati who lack male role models. They hold an annual car wash to pay for the year's activities. Community service is integrated into courses such as the social justice/American history course.

The school boasts of its success in both athletics and academics. More than half of its Division One athletic teams have won state championships, and it has frequently had the most National Merit semifinalists in the city.

Noted Alumni

Jim Bunning, U.S. senator for Kentucky and former MLB pitcher
John Diehl, actor
Joseph Hudepohl, former Olympic swimmer
Kevin Kern, Broadway actor
Simon Leis, sheriff of Hamilton County

— IHS —

Scranton Preparatory School

Location: Scranton, Pennsylvania
Founded: 1944
Number of Students: 800
Student Body: Coed
Nickname: Cavaliers

Interesting Information

Scranton Prep was founded as a division of the University of Scranton but received its own charter in 1977. Originally all-male, it became coed in 1971 in order to serve girls from Marywood Seminary, a girls school run by the Immaculate Heart of Mary sisters, whose building burned down.

Scranton Prep has been upgrading and expanding its campus. Its original building once housed a correspondence school. In recent years, it raised fourteen million dollars to build an arts and sciences building and a new athletic center. It prides itself on being the premier college preparatory school in northeast Pennsylvania and on a service program that requires all students to donate one hundred hours, half in their senior year. Options for service include participating in a service trip to an orphanage in Mexico.

Noted Alumni

P. J. Carlesimo, assistant coach of the San Antonio Spurs
Robert Casey, former governor of Pennsylvania
Bob Casey Jr., U.S. senator for Pennsylvania
Glynn Lunney, former manager and flight director for NASA
John A. Walsh, senior vice president and executive editor of ESPN

Seattle Preparatory School

Location: Seattle, Washington
Founded: 1891
Number of Students: 690
Student Body: Coed
Nickname: Panthers

Interesting Information

Seattle Prep occupies a seven-acre campus in the historic Capitol Hill neighborhood. In the 1930s, it separated from Seattle University, but in 1973, Jesuits and their lay associates found a way to unite the two schools again—in Matteo Ricci College. The prestigious Academy for Educational Development has hailed this as "one of the twelve most successful educational innovations" in the nation.

Matteo Ricci College, named in honor of a sixteenth-century Jesuit missionary to China, allows juniors to leave Seattle Prep a year early and move directly to Seattle University, where they can receive a bachelor's degree in another three years. The key to the program's success is not the fact that students can finish both high school and college in six years, but its "integrated" curriculum, which connects religion, history, and English. Matteo Ricci College has received awards from the Carnegie Foundation, the U.S. Department of Education, and the Richfield Foundation. It is the reason that some students choose Seattle Prep.

Noted Alumni

David Kennedy, historian
Greg Nickels, mayor of Seattle
Martell Webster, guard for the Portland Trail Blazers

— IHS —

Strake Jesuit College Preparatory

Location: Houston, Texas
Founded: 1961
Number of Students: 870
Student Body: All-male
Nickname: Crusaders

Interesting Information

Strake Jesuit College Preparatory gained national attention in 2005 when it created a "school within a school" for New Orleans Jesuit High School victims of Hurricane Katrina, but that wasn't the school's first brush with a hurricane. Hurricane Carla delayed Strake Jesuit's opening in 1961.

Strake Jesuit occupies a campus-like setting that includes a new athletic complex, the Johnny Keane Field House, the Lowman Theater, a technology building, and classroom buildings. The Moody Memorial Library houses the Strake Jesuit Art Museum, featuring the works of Picasso, Henry Moore, and others.

In 1974, Strake Jesuit became one of the first schools in Texas to require service for seniors. Since then, it has added service opportunities for sophomores and juniors. The goal is "for each person in our school family to understand the responsibility of putting faith into action, to experience the joy of serving Christ in the needy and poor among us, and to follow Christ's call to build a world grounded in faith and justice."

University of Detroit Jesuit High School and Academy

Location: Detroit, Michigan
Founded: 1877
Number of Students: 840 (grades 7–12)
Student Body: All-male
Nickname: Cubs

Interesting Information

In 1975, University of Detroit Jesuit High School and Academy committed itself to remaining within the city of Detroit rather than move to a suburb. Since then, it has become one of the area's most ethnically and socioeconomically diverse schools, in addition to being Detroit's oldest continuously functioning high school. The total student body includes 112 seventh and eighth graders enrolled in the academy, who are becoming prepared for the rigors of a Jesuit high school. The school provides more than one million dollars in tuition assistance a year.

University of Detroit Jesuit High School students serve their community. For more than thirty years, they have received weekly class time for service under the guidance of a faculty member. Through their work with Detroit's Focus: HOPE (a civil and human rights organization), they participate in monthly food deliveries, a holiday adopt-a-family program, and a freshman service day. In addition to working with organizations like Focus: HOPE, Detroit Jesuit students go on service missions to South Carolina, Honduras, and Guatemala. The school boasts of its strong athletic programs and the number of National Merit semifinalists it produces.

Noted Alumni

Michael Cavanagh, justice of the Michigan Supreme Court
Gus Johnson, announcer for CBS Sports
Elmore Leonard, novelist and screenwriter
Michael Moriarty, actor
Ron Rice, former NFL safety

— IHS —

Verbum Dei High School

Location: Los Angeles, California
Founded: 1962
Number of Students: 340
Student Body: All-male
Nickname: Eagles

Interesting Information

The Missionaries of the Society of the Divine Word founded Verbum Dei in 1962 to serve African American and Latino boys in the Watts area of Los Angeles. For years, the school was a beacon for its depressed neighborhood, but it declined as the religious order lost members. To save it from closing, the Jesuits agreed to cosponsor the school with the Archdiocese of Los Angeles, adopting the Cristo Rey work-study model to allow students to pay half of their tuition. Charitable foundations help parents pay the remainder.

The school prepares students for the workplace with courses in computing and business etiquette. Students view the work-study program, along with Verbum Dei's academic program, as their ticket to a better life. Graduates have fulfilled all requirements for admission to California state schools and most colleges in the United States, in addition to completing religion courses.

— IHS —

Walsh Jesuit High School

Location: Cuyahoga Falls, Ohio
Founded: 1965

Number of Students: 950
Student Body: Coed
Nickname: Warriors

Interesting Information

Walsh Jesuit High School owes its founding to the generosity of the Cuyahoga Falls family for which it is named. Jane Walsh, wife of Cornelius Walsh, and her nephew William A. Walsh spent years trying to persuade various bishops and Jesuit provincials to use a large bequest to start the school. By the time the Detroit Province agreed to do so, the bequest had grown to nearly two million dollars, further supplemented by a one-million-dollar gift from the Cleveland diocese. The school opened in 1965 on farmland near Cuyahoga Falls.

The school draws strong support from grateful alums. James M. Allwin, class of '70, founder and president of Aetos Capital LLC, has been the largest donor to a ten-million-dollar capital campaign to build an entry and administrative wings, a fine arts center, and a fitness center, to renovate the commons, and to expand the chapel. "I really believe in giving back, especially because Walsh Jesuit was such an important part of my life," he says. "Walsh Jesuit graduates should reflect on their time at the school and know they benefited from the generosity of so many who came before them." Walsh Jesuit attracts students from more than one hundred grade schools in seven counties. It has twice been named a Blue Ribbon School of Excellence by the U.S. Department of Education.

Noted Alumni

James M. Allwin, founder and president of Aetos Capital LLC
Chris Connor, chairman and CEO of the Sherwin-Williams
    Company

— IHS —

Xavier High School

Location: New York, New York
Founded: 1847
Number of Students: 950
Student Body: All-male
Nickname: Knights

Interesting Information

Xavier High School, located in the Chelsea neighborhood of Manhattan, began as the College of St. Francis Xavier and had its own graduate school. In the 1880s, it became a Jesuit military day school. Its precision drill team, the X-Squad, competes all over the country and has taken top rankings at Army Nationals. Although Junior ROTC has been optional since 1971, it remains a major school activity. Xavier High cadets march in the annual Columbus Day and St. Patrick's Day parades.

Xavier seniors work with numerous organizations serving children, the homeless, the elderly, and the disabled. Students also participate in both area service and international service trips.

Noted Alumni

Dave Anderson, sportswriter for the *New York Times*
Fr. Walter Burghardt, SJ, preacher and writer
Fr. John Courtney Murray, SJ, theologian
Al Roker, weather anchor for *The Today Show*
Antonin Scalia, associate justice of the U.S. Supreme Court

Epilogue: A Look at the Future

As the 2006–07 school year was about to open, Jesuit high schools nationwide were booming. Despite rising tuition costs, enrollments were generally at capacity. Many schools could accept only a percentage of applicants. School Web sites displayed pictures of improved facilities and technology, and the "News" links boasted of academic and athletic achievements, many publicized in local media.

Yet the schools face challenges to maintain their traditional excellence. Dr. Bernard Bouillette, vice president of the Jesuit Secondary Education Association, reflected on the current state of Jesuit high school education and what the future may hold for the schools.

What is your overall assessment of the state of the nation's Jesuit high schools?
Overall, the state of Jesuit schools is very healthy. Schools are vibrant, programs are expanding, enrollment strong.

What are their greatest strengths?
The greatest strengths lie in the implementation of the Jesuit mission and Ignatian vision by talented, qualified, and dedicated professionals working in partnership with committed families in a tradition supported by alumni and local communities. The schools set high expectations and provide quality programs and support services to meet those expectations, with a focus on the growth of the whole person—intellectually, spiritually, and socially. The care for the individual remains a hallmark of Jesuit schools, and this care shows itself in many ways, but hopefully there is a place for every student to fit

in, to be challenged, to be respected with the opportunity to grow, and to succeed.

Jesuit schools receive tremendous support from their alumni and their local communities. Many schools throughout the country have recently completed or are in the process of beginning major capital campaigns, with considerable improvements to facilities, programs, and endowments.

What are their greatest challenges?

The greatest challenges include

- Continuing strong leadership in the future
- Fostering Jesuit and Ignatian identity
- Building endowments
- Attracting and retaining lower- and middle-class families
- Providing continued professional development for faculty and staff that includes adult spiritual formation with an emphasis on Ignatian spirituality
- Retaining quality faculty and staff
- Developing and evaluating curricula that support the Jesuit mission of the schools

A few critics seem to believe that terms like "men and women for others" are just marketing slogans. They want alums to work for major social change. What is your response?

The father general of the Society of Jesus, Fr. Peter-Hans Kolvenbach, SJ, has suggested that the motto be revised to include "and with" between the "for" and "others." Yes, the mottoes can become overused and even poorly used, but they serve to remind all of us that we have an obligation to build community, to give and receive, to address the need of our communities and world, especially those who are marginalized. We work for peace and justice to the degree that we are able and within the context of our life situations. Our education is for a purpose—to help ourselves and others save souls—and we realize this at different times in our lives. We learn this differently, and sometimes we get it when we're in school and sometimes many years later. We sow the seeds!

Although the number of Jesuits in the schools has dropped drastically in the past thirty years, there are still a few at most of the schools. What will happen when some schools have none? Will they be able to maintain their Jesuit identity?

As long as the mission of the Society of Jesus and that of the schools is clear and the characteristics of a Jesuit education are in place, with clear methods to evaluate and develop those characteristics, the Jesuit identity will continue to thrive. Jesuit and lay leadership have been strong in our Jesuit high schools for many years. Schools have been developing professional development and curricular programs that support the Jesuit mission and Ignatian vision with greater intentionality. St. Ignatius wrote that it was the charge of Jesuits to start good works in a place, empower people to assume responsibility for those works, and then move on. We are getting to experience what that really means in our schools, but it has not been a sudden awareness. The Society of Jesus in its last General Congregation called on Jesuits to embrace this collaboration. The partnership of the Society and lay leaders is seriously addressed as provinces support their apostolates. The JSEA and its programs have provided many opportunities for this collaboration to become a reality through seminars, symposia, and colloquia.

Jesuit high schools are strong, traditional institutions that were hit hard about thirty years ago by confusion in identity, a decline in the number of Jesuit Scholastics and Jesuits on faculties, falling

enrollments, etc. Now they seem to have come back stronger than ever. How do you explain this?

I attribute this to the founding of the Jesuit Secondary Education Association and the work of this association and its commissions over the past twenty-five years. The Jesuit schools that make up JSEA have focused attention on and developed programs to promote the Jesuit mission and Ignatian vision. I think that one characteristic of Jesuit apostolates is that they are free to discern the needs of the times as they change and to discern God's plan in those changing times.

Jesuit high schools are currently raising at least four hundred million dollars in capital/endowment campaigns alone. Are alumni likely to remain as loyal and generous in the future with a reduced Jesuit presence in most of the schools?

This is hard to answer, but alumni support is still strong, with young alumni who may not have experienced many individual Jesuits in their own educations. I believe that Jesuit high school seniors of today graduate with as strong an identification with and affection for their schools as ever and that these traits bode well for future support.

As mentioned earlier, the capital campaigns of many schools have been extremely successful, and new campaigns are planned in many schools. The feasibility studies conducted before all these drives indicate strong support among alumni and friends of the schools.

Were the Jesuit schools affected by the clerical scandals in terms of bad PR, loss of donations, etc.?

All of us have been affected by the scandals in a dispiriting way. However, the Jesuit schools have for the most part attempted to address these scandals openly, with care and concern for all involved. On the national level, school enrollments continue to grow, fund-raising continues to expand, new schools are opening.

It appears that most of the schools that converted from all-male to coed did so in the 1970s and 1980s to stabilize enrollment and solve financial problems. With most schools having competitive enrollment, is the era of going coed over?
With many schools facing full enrollment, this may be the case. However, Loyola Academy [in Wilmette, Illinois] went coed in 1994 for philosophical reasons and for purposes of providing Catholic education options for young women in that area of the North Shore of Chicago. Regis, in the Denver area, went co-institutional four years ago to address the needs of young Catholic women in that region. All new Cristo Rey schools affiliated with the Society of Jesus that have opened in the last few years are coeducational. I don't think that the era is over, but it will change.

Conversely, what is the continuing appeal of single-sex education?
Tradition and the perception that some students learn better in single-sex environments. The research is very mixed, except for students from low socioeconomic families. There are many people who believe that it is easier to focus on the gender-related developmental needs of students in a single-gender environment.

What is your personal opinion of single-sex versus coed Jesuit education? Does JSEA encourage or discourage either option?
JSEA does not encourage or discourage either choice. As a service organization, JSEA serves the needs of the member and associate member schools and does not prescribe programs and policies. As for myself, I

believe it is a strength to have options for families—there are benefits for single-sex and coed options, and those benefits vary for different children. I have worked in both situations and have truly enjoyed both. My own blood, sweat, and tears, however, went toward a transition to coeducation, so I might be a bit biased. Gender-related development needs may be addressed in both contexts given the appropriate intentionality and staff and curriculum development.

What is the significance of the Cristo Rey schools? They are spreading rapidly. What cities are planning Jesuit-sponsored Cristo Rey schools?

The significance of these schools is that they have successfully forged a partnership among lower-income families, schools, and the business community, with a win-win experience for all. As many of these schools are also affiliated with the Society of Jesus, the number of Jesuit schools is increasing at a fairly rapid rate, and that's quite significant. At least three new Jesuit-sponsored Cristo Rey schools are in the planning stages—in Baltimore, Minneapolis, and Newark—in addition to others affiliated with dioceses or other religious orders. Eventually, there could be other Jesuit-sponsored or cosponsored Cristo Rey schools.

What do you think Jesuit schools will be like ten years from now? What changes will we see?

I do not have a crystal ball, and ten years is a long time. I think there will be some changes, but the roots and the trunk will change little. We will see more lay leaders in Jesuit schools and perhaps more laywomen. We know there will continue to be fewer Jesuits. The question will be Where is the best place for those Jesuits to exercise their unique role and contribution? It may not always be as president.

I hope that we will continue to make progress in realizing Jesuit-lay collaboration as real partnership in actions as well as words. I think we will continue to see an increased focus on the Society's mission and school mission. I also think that the spiritual-formation and Christian service programs will continue to become more integrated within the curriculum of the schools. Schools will be continuously more intentional in all that they do in support of the mission.

Also, I hope that in ten years there will be a national policy in place for the sponsorship of Jesuit schools by the Society of Jesus as well as standardized methods for accountability.

All in all, then, it sounds like you think that Jesuit high schools are going to be going strong for the next generation—and probably still tormenting their athletic rivals to boot. Right?
Right!

Acknowledgments

....

This book reflects the help and support of many people. In writing this catalog of thanks, I fear leaving off someone who should be named, since virtually everyone I contacted was more than generous with his or her time and assistance. My apologies to anyone I have omitted, but here are many of those to whom I am indebted.

Jesuit Secondary Education Association

Fr. Joe O'Connell, SJ, endorsed my first, vague idea for the book and promised JSEA's support. Dr. Bernie Bouillette was ever helpful when "that pest in Omaha" called or e-mailed him (frequently) for assistance. Fr. Ralph Metts, SJ, spent valuable time during his first weeks at a new job helping me tie together the themes of this book.

Creighton Prep

Fr. Tom Merkel, SJ, was a gold mine of information about Jesuit high schools from his time as president of the JSEA board and explained their commonalities. Jeff Hausman provided names of his peers in development and promotion at other schools and encouragement at every turn. Mike Pietro, former alumni director, provided initial artwork for the cover. David Laughlin is president of St. Louis University High, but I'm going to thank him with Creighton Prep friends, because that is where I met him. I assumed that anyone who did a stellar job of administering Jesuit-style discipline could explain it, and he did, wonderfully. Fr. Jim Michalski, SJ, of the Jesuit Middle School of Omaha, explained the Prep retreat that he created.

I am grateful to Prep for my son's Jesuit education and for introducing me to the world of Jesuit high schools. I had to resist the temptation to turn this into a Creighton Prep book.

Creighton University

Thanks to all of my Jesuit colleagues, especially Fr. Larry Gillick, SJ, who gave me a crash course in Ignatian spirituality, suggested sources, allowed me to tag along on his retreat for Fordham Prep, and read the chapter on Ignatian spirituality. Fr. Andy Alexander, SJ, a former board president of Creighton Prep, explained the relationship between Ignatian spirituality and Jesuit high school education and guided me in shaping the book. Fr. Don Doll, SJ, my colleague and friend and a world-class photographer, donated the cover photo of the St. Ignatius statue. Fr. Ray Bucko, SJ, drove me to Red Cloud High (an eight-hour drive) and provided insights into the school and Lakota culture. A faculty seminar on Ignatian identity funded by academic vice president Christine Wiseman was extremely beneficial. Thanks to those who worked on it, including my friends Dr. Tim Cook and Fr. Roc O'Connor, SJ (of St. Louis Jesuits fame).

I also want to thank Mary Nash, reference librarian par excellence, who did the initial literature search, showing how little had been written about Jesuit schools, and colleagues in the Department of Journalism and Mass Communication, especially Ann McDonald, for their patience with me as I worked on this project.

Provincial Assistants for Secondary Education

The provincial assistants for secondary education were *the* keys to finding great interviews and stories from schools nationwide. I am especially indebted to Fr. Jim Stoeger, SJ, of the Chicago Province; Fr. Donald Petkash, SJ, of the Detroit Province; Art Zinselmeyer, of the Missouri Province; and John Raslowsky, of the New York Province for their invaluable assistance in explaining specific aspects of Jesuit high schools and suggesting school and individual profile subjects. They also provided overview interviews for chapters. Fr. Stoeger even drove me around Chicago. Many thanks!

Other Colleagues

Colleagues from the AJCU Communications Conference and the *Company* magazine board provided input and assistance. Fr. Paul Campbell, SJ, of Loyola Press helped me shape my proposal to Loyola Press and vouched for my credibility. Fr. Mark Thibodeaux, SJ, then of Strake Jesuit High School, encouraged me to write this book, offered great suggestions on topics and sources, and arranged my visit to Strake Jesuit as it hosted New Orleans Jesuit after Katrina. Dr. Bren Murphy, of Loyola University Chicago, suggested using photos and offered helpful reactions to my plans and text. Fr. Paul Soukup, SJ, of Santa Clara University encouraged me to visit St. Ignatius Prep in San Francisco and said I *had* to profile Br. Doug Draper, SJ. Fr. Walter Deye, SJ, president of St. Xavier High School, explained the growth of collaboration with lay leaders. Fr. Thomas Widner, SJ, rector of the Jesuit community at Brebeuf, gave excellent insights into that unique school.

School Facilitators/Hosts

School facilitators and hosts enabled me to maximize my short time at the schools I visited by setting up interviews for me. I am grateful to all: Paul Totah, of St. Ignatius Prep in San Francisco; Fr. Peter Klink, SJ, and Tina Merdanian, of Red Cloud High School; Courtney Mikoryak, of Brebeuf Jesuit Preparatory School; Peter Beale-DelVecchio and Fr. Jim Gartland, SJ, of Cristo Rey Jesuit High School; Michael Howell and Fr. Allen Novotny, SJ, of Gonzaga College High School;

Michael Heringer, of Rockhurst High School; and Chiara Wrocinski, of St. Ignatius College Prep in Chicago. Thanks also to Jim and LeeAnn Badum for hosting me in Houston.

I am indebted to Paul Hogan, of Jesuit High School in Portland, for explaining Ignatian pedagogy and suggesting good sources. Alumni, development, and promotion officials who were especially helpful included Nick Suszynski, of Jesuit High School of Tampa; John Prael, of Regis High School in New York; and Daniel Costello, of Gonzaga College High School.

Loyola Press

I have greatly enjoyed working with the talented people of Loyola Press, especially my content editor, Jim Manney, who answered all questions cheerfully, brainstormed with me through difficulties, and then did a splendid job of improving my copy. I'm also grateful to acquisitions editor Joe Durepos, as well as Michelle Halm and Carrie Freyer, marketing coordinators, and Heidi Hill, editor, for making this project fun as well as rewarding.

Finally, I want to thank members of my family, especially my mother, Kathleen McGowen Wirth, to whom this book is dedicated. She acted interested in my daily e-mails outlining progress, asked good questions about drafts, and voiced enthusiasm. I'm grateful to my nephew David Wirth for driving me to San Francisco and patiently listening to a full day of interviews. Thanks to my sister, Janet Poley, for organizing the trip to Washington, DC, that allowed me to visit Gonzaga College High School. My children, Raj and Shanti Psota, gave me love and support, as did my brother, Mark Wirth, and my other siblings and my cousins Marylou Garrett and John Wirth.

I am especially indebted to my friends Liz Sundem and Jeanne Weeks for cheerfully listening to my unending descriptions of what I was doing on the book and even asking for such updates. We really do get along with a little help from our friends—or a lot!

Bibliography

Books

Angell, Roger. *A Pitcher's Story: Innings with David Cone.* New York: Warner Books, 2001.

Aschenbrenner, George A. *Stretched for Greater Glory: What to Expect from the Spiritual Exercises.* Chicago: Loyola Press, 2004.

Callahan, John J. *Discovering a Sacred World.* John J. Callahan, 1997.

Conroy, Pat. *My Losing Season.* New York: Nan A. Talese, 2002.

Currie, Elliott. *The Road to Whatever: Middle-Class Culture and the Crisis of Adolescence.* New York: Metropolitan Books, 2004.

Dezell, Maureen. *Irish America: Coming into Clover.* New York: Anchor Books, 2002.

Donnelly, John Patrick. *Ignatius of Loyola: Founder of the Jesuits.* Library of World Biography series. New York: Pearson Education, 2004.

Fremon, Celeste. *Father Greg and the Homeboys: The Extraordinary Journey of Father Greg Boyle and His Work with the Latino Gangs of East L.A.* New York: Hyperion, 1995.

Gurian, Michael, and Kathy Stevens. *The Minds of Boys: Saving Our Sons from Falling Behind in School and Life.* San Francisco: Jossey-Bass, 2005.

Hansen, Ron. *A Stay against Confusion: Essays on Faith and Fiction.* New York: HarperCollins, 2001.

Ignatius of Loyola. *The Autobiography of St. Ignatius Loyola.* Edited by John C. Olin. Translated by Joseph F. O'Callaghan. New York: Harper & Row, 1974.

_____. *The Spiritual Exercises of Saint Ignatius.* Translated by Pierre Wolff. Liguori, MO: Triumph, 1997.

Jesuit Conference in the United States of America. *What Makes a Jesuit School Jesuit?* 2007.

Lowney, Chris. *Heroic Leadership: Best Practices from a 450-Year-Old Company That Changed the World.* Chicago: Loyola Press, 2003.

Martin, James. *My Life with the Saints.* Chicago: Loyola Press, 2006.

McDonough, Peter and Eugene C. Bianchi. *Passionate Uncertainty: Inside the American Jesuits.* Berkeley: University of California Press, 2002.

McGinley, Phyllis. *Saint-Watching.* New York: Crossroad, 1982.

McGloin, Joseph T. *I'll Die Laughing.* Milwaukee: Bruce, 1955.

_____. *Smile at Your Own Risk.* Milwaukee: Bruce, 1959.

McGough, Matthew. *Bat Boy: My True Life Adventures Coming of Age with the New York Yankees.* New York: Doubleday, 2005.

Metts, Ralph E. *Ignatius Knew.* Washington, DC: Jesuit Secondary Education Association, 1995.

Modras, Ronald. *Ignatian Humanism: A Dynamic Spirituality for the 21st Century.* Chicago: Loyola Press, 2004.

Muldoon, Tim. *The Ignatian Workout: Daily Spiritual Exercises for a Healthy Faith.* Chicago: Loyola Press, 2004.

O'Malley, John W. *The First Jesuits.* Cambridge, MA: Harvard University Press, 1993.

O'Malley, John W., John W. Padberg, and Vincent T. O'Keefe. *Jesuit Spirituality: A Now and Future Resource.* Chicago: Loyola University Press, 1990.

Padberg, John. "Development of the Ratio Studiorum." In *The Jesuit Ratio Studiorum: 400th Anniversary Perspectives,* edited by Vincent J. Duminuco, 80–100. New York: Fordham University Press, 2000.

Pipher, Mary. *Writing to Change the World.* New York: Riverhead Books, 2006.

Rahner, Karl. *The Church and the Sacraments.* Translated by W. J. O'Hara. New York: Herder and Herder, 1963.

Russert, Tim. *Big Russ & Me: Father and Son, Lessons of Life.* New York: Miramax Books, 2004.

Totah, Paul. *Spiritus Magis: 150 Years of St. Ignatius College Preparatory.* San Francisco: St. Ignatius College Preparatory, 2005.

Traub, George W., SJ. *Do You Speak Ignatian?* Cincinnati: Xavier University, 2004.

Wirth, Eileen. *Effective Catholic High School Public Relations: A Book of Cases.* Washington, DC: National Catholic Educational Association, 2003.

Articles

Aksamit, Nicole. "Running on Faith." *Omaha World-Herald,* November 2, 2004.

Belcher, Walt. "From the Beginning to Best Series Finale, PBS Captures Essence of Bob Newhart." *Tampa Tribune,* July 18, 2005.

Carter, John. "Coach." *Company*, 1987.

Flanigan, James. "Firms Offering Students the Benefit of Experience." *Los Angeles Times*, June 20, 2004.

Goode, Jon. "'Easy Ed' Played the Game Hard." *Boston.com*, April 14, 2005, http://www.boston.com/sports/basketball/celtics/articles/2005/04/14/easy_ed_played_the_game_hard/.

Haight, Abby. "A Portland Rower Hopes to Turn Silver into Gold." *Oregonian*, October 17, 2004.

———. "Their Work Is Child's Play." *Oregonian*, July 18, 2006.

Hanchin, Timothy. "Messianic or Bourgeois?" *America*, May 8, 2006.

Johnson, Kate. "Congratulations and Welcome Home." *Age Quod Agis*, Winter 2005.

Lankenau, Tom. "Touched by the Flame." *Company*, Winter 2005.

Lausch, Carolyn. "A Privileged Moment: Teachers and Learners Walking the Way of Ignatius." Jesuit Secondary Education Association, http://www.jsea.org (downloaded January 2, 2006).

Mathews, Jay. "Small School's Idea Holds Great Promise." *Washington Post*, March 4, 2003.

Meuler, Greg. "50 Years of Education: Changes and Challenges in Jesuit Secondary Education; From Blackrobes to Robes of Many Colors." *Jesuit Journeys*, Spring/Summer 2005.

"Mission Impossible." *Creighton Prep Alumni News*, Summer 2006.

"Most Likely to Succeed." *Company,* Fall 2004.

Nero, Phil. "Jesuit Callings." *Creighton Prep Alumni News*, Winter 2006.

Palmer, Ann Therese. "Cristo Rey Crafts a School Model That Works." *Chicago Tribune*, December 26, 2003.

Pavur, Claud. "A Masterful Plan." *Company*, Fall 2005.

Rhodes, Marion. "Teens Put Others First in Massive Operation." *Omaha World-Herald*, December 19, 2005.

Ryan, Katie. "Students Still Tied to Life on the Reservation." *Creightonian*, November 11, 2005.

Schemo, Diana Jean. "Charities Pledge $19 Million to Jesuit Model Schools." *New York Times*, May 21, 2003.

Seipp, Catherine. "No Sideshow Bob." *National Review*, July 19, 2005, http://www.nationalreview.com/seipp/seipp200507190737.asp.

Smith, Robert L. "Student Group Eases Burden at Funerals." *Cleveland Plain Dealer*, November 11, 2005.

Stickney, Dane. "He Wants Students to Have All the Credit." *Omaha World-Herald*, December 20, 2005.

Sullivan, Rick. "The Best of Both Worlds." *Company*, Spring 2005.

Szalewski, Susan. "A Little Party for a Thrifty Man." *Omaha World-Herald*, August 16, 2004 (accessed from LexisNexis on June 22, 2005).

Trimble, Charles. "Mission School Remembered." *Indian Country Today*, September 2, 2003. http://www.indiancountry.com (accessed on February 27, 2006).

Vander Ark, Tom. "New Educational Options." *America*, October 27, 2003.

"Verbum Dei High School: Work Study Program Has Students Working for Their Futures." *Los Angeles Business Journal,* September 29, 2003.

Wirth, Eileen. "A Family Album." *Company*, Spring 2005.

————. "Social Justice Philosophy Plays Out in Wake of Gulf Hurricanes." *Momentum*, February/March 2006.

Documents

Society of Jesus. *General Council 34*, decree 13, no. 4.

Major Interviews by the Author

Alexander, Andy, SJ. May 20, 2005.

Beale-DelVecchio, Peter. May 5, 2006.

Bouillette, Bernard. February 6, 2006.

Carr, Mark, SJ. January 27, 2006.

Costello, Daniel. June 23, 2006.

Deye, Walter, SJ. August 9, 2006.

Draper, Douglas, SJ. October 20, 2005.

Ferlita, Casey, SJ. November 18, 2005.

Gartland, Jim, SJ. May 5, 2005.

Gillick, Larry, SJ. June 2, 2005 and September 22, 2005.

Grady, Tim. August 10, 2006.

Heringer, Michael. March 31, 2006.

Hils, Steve. August 10, 2006.

Hogan, Paul. February 6, 2006.

Homer, Paul. September 23, 2005.

Howell, Michael. June 23, 2006.

Klink, Peter, SJ. January 27, 2006.

Klosner, Gene. June 23, 2005.

Lahart, Daniel, SJ. November 18, 2005.

Laughlin, David. November 22, 2005.

Markey, Earle, SJ. June 29, 2006.

Merdanian, Tina. January 27, 2006.

Merkel, Thomas, SJ, and Jeffrey Hausman. May 31, 2005.

Metts, Ralph, SJ. August 11, 2006.

Novotny, Allen, SJ. June 23, 2006.

O'Connell, Joseph, SJ. March 29, 2005.

O'Hagan, Michael. July 10, 2006.

Petkash, Don, SJ. March 13, 2006.

Quesnell, Dan. August 9, 2006.

Raslowsky, John. March 21, 2006.

Sauer, Anthony P., SJ. October 20, 2005.

Steele, Ann. August 10, 2006.

Stoeger, James, SJ. December 8, 2005.

Thibodeaux, Mark, SJ. November 18, 2005.

White Eyes, Roger. January 27, 2006.

Widner, Thomas, SJ. February 10, 2006.

Wrocinski, Chiara. May 5, 2006.

Zinselmeyer, Art. January 17, 2006.

Web Sites

Gonzaga College High School: http://www.gonzaga.org.

Basketball Hall of Fame: http://www.hoophall.com.

Jesuit High School, New Orleans: http://www.jesuitnola.org.

Jesuit Secondary Education Association: http://www.jsea.org.

St. Louis Walk of Fame: http://www.stlouiswalkoffame.org.

Villa la Paz: http://www.villalapazfoundation.org.